JUST BEYOND THE BRIDGE

JUST BEYOND THE BRIDGE

ELLEN H. LINDSEY

JUST BEYOND THE BRIDGE

ISBN: 978-1-365-67170-8

Photography: Atiba Sonnebeyatta

Cover Design: Kevin L. Knox

Editors: Edith Susie Pagan and Joelle Wagner-Lynch

Dedication

My wife, Tanisha L. Williams-Lindsey

My sons, William K. Valentine Jr. and Maurice L. Matthews

My parents who raised me, Mr. & Mrs. Walter Lindsey

My birth parents, Cliff Etheridge 'Junebug' Campbell and Laverene Pyatt

My brothers, Ricardo Pagan and Duan Pyatt

My work wife, Fatimah Shakir

Table of Contents

Chapter 1
Untold Truths

My journey of 50 years has revealed some lies. Born in Elizabeth NJ, as the only child to my mother, brought home to Scotch Plains NJ, and at the age of 9 moved to Plainfield NJ. Prior to moving to Plainfield, I attended a private school which I hated. I had no friends, the teachers did not like me, and I did not like them. I remember one day my teacher sent a note home for my parents over the weekend. I returned to school Monday, and the teacher asked where the note was. Of course, I'm looking dumbfounded because I never gave my parents the note. She called home, and Lord knows I did not want to go home after school. When I got home, I gave my parents the note that was the first time my dad beat me; he beat me with the belt buckle and, I had bruises for days. It was also the last time he beat me. Thinking back, I did pull another stunt. I was bussed to school. That afternoon I did not want to go home. To this day, I couldn't tell you the reason why, but I told the bus driver I wanted to ride with him to all the stops. My parents were so worried about me. I remember getting home close to 5pm. My parents met me while getting off the bus. My dad was furious with the bus driver. No, lie I can't remember if I got in trouble or not, I just know they were happy to see me. After this stunt my parents transferred me to a catholic school. It was worse than attending school in Scotch Plains. The teachers and I had personality conflicts. At the time I still did not have friends and my grades were terrible. Finally, I told my aunt who is my mom's sister and my favorite aunt that I hated catholic school and wanted to attend public school. My aunt discussed it with my mom and told her how I felt. My mom asked me why I did not tell her. I replied because I didn't think you would transfer me out of the school.

My parents sold our house in Scotch Plains, and we moved to Plainfield. Moving here a was little better. The neighborhood had children who I can play with. I still wouldn't't say we were real friends, but they occupied my time well. I started attending Cedarbrook Elementary School, by this time I was in the sixth grade. Now what's interesting about this is, when I walked into class, I saw a few of same girls who bullied when I attended the catholic school, and what's even funnier is one of the girls is on my Facebook page till this day. I just couldn't't catch a break. I never could understand why females and I couldn't't just be friends, or better yet, why I couldn't't make friends. I guess there was something about me that was simply different. I did find as I got older, I was comfortable around boys. Except for this one dude in my sixth-grade class. I remember he was skinny as a toothpick! One day he wanted to show off in front of the class. He was getting smart with me, making jokes trying to embarrass me saying he was going to beat my ass. I said a few choice words towards back at him. There are two important things I remember about that day he told me "Don't write a check your ass can't cash". Of course, most of the class had their money on him. The end of the day came, the bell rung, and everyone was running outside to see this fight. Well, all I'm going to say is I cashed that check. After beating his ass, I ran home and told my mom what happened. I didn't get suspended, but I think I had detention the next day. After I proved myself and my skills, I didn't have to worry about people bothering me again.

It seems my parents have a thing for secrets. I remember while still living in Scotch Plains, my mom found out my dad had two daughters living in Florida. My oldest sister got in contact with my mom and informed her my dad has two daughters from his previous marriage who live in Florida. One afternoon my mom asked my dad did he have other children besides my brother Toni whom she knew about, my dad said no. My mom asked him the same question several times, and each time he denied having or knowing about having other children. Finally, my mom went and got her gun and threatened to blow my dad's asshole out if he didn't tell her the truth. After a few minutes of waving that gun around at him He then admitted to having two daughters who lived in Florida from his first marriage.

Joyce came to NJ to meet us. She was tall, thin, beautiful, and intelligent. She spent a couple of days with us. She was able to ask my dad questions that she needed answers to. After her visit, my mom decided we would fly to Tampa, Florida on Christmas day to meet my other sister Frances and the rest of the family. We stayed until New Year's Eve. As we were getting ready to return home, Frances went into labor. Unfortunately, she couldn't see us off to the airport. She was admitted into the hospital about to give birth to my now nephew who she gave my father's first name. This was our only visit to see my siblings and their family in Florida as a family.

Before my parents were blessed with me, my mom had four miscarriages. This is the reason why my middle name is Hope. My mom stated she hoped so long to have a child, and when I came along, she felt God answered her prayers.

JUST BEYOND THE BRIDGE

Growing up I don't remember my mother showing affection, but she did spoil me. In my eyes my parents were both strict. My dad was calm and mean, and my mom was no-nonsense. I guess that was her way of being loving. I was more of a daddy's girl. I loved my daddy. Although he was evil as hell, we could relate. My mom always said I have a lot of his ways. My dad had a way of responding to people which I always thought was mean. My mom said he was too evil for anyone else to want him. He didn't like people much, but people had a way of gravitating to my dad. My dad didn't hang out. He always came home after work, and was around his family, whether it be us, or the in-laws who lived in Newark, who then moved to Irvington, NJ. That was the extension of my dad going somewhere or hanging with friends.

My dad's favorite saying was "I don't need a living ass". I adopted that saying which became my slogan for years, which I really believed. My dad worked nights, and my mom was a housewife. My dad was a good provider for our family. We didn't want for much. The one fault my dad had with me was he could not keep his promises. All the kids in the neighborhood had skates, they would be outside roller skating, and I would be watching. I asked my dad to buy me a pair. He told me he would, but never did. Until this day, I never learned to skate. Another promise my dad broke was for my sixteen birthday. I asked each parent for a specific amount of money. My mom came through with her half, but my dad didn't have his. I remember being in my room crying like a baby, I was so hurt. This was my finalization to not liking birthday's.   My parents planned for me to have a sweet sixteen party. Unfortunately, it was a major snowstorm on that day, and my party was canceled. Maybe God knew no one was coming and was sparing my feelings with the storm. You see, this was the second attempt to have a birthday party. At the age of six my parents were giving me a birthday party after church on that Sunday. My mom told me people had to go home and change out of there church close before arriving. Then suddenly, it started snowing which became a major snowstorm. My mom said I cried, and she tried showing me the snow, but I just couldn't't understand it was a severe snowstorm. Because of these events, I stopped celebrating my birthday in my birth month. March of 2020 was the first time in years, I celebrated my birthday on its actual date. Thank God my wife planned it before COVID 19 shut everything down. As I recall the following week New Jersey was shut down and quarantined. Prior to that was my fortieth birthday, which my ex-wife threw me a surprise birthday party on the boat Spirit of Philadelphia. For all these reasons I celebrate my birthday in warm months like April, and August. It's interesting how little things can affect you mentally throughout your adult life.

Now my mom didn't have too many friends either. She spent her time with her sister, and brothers. She spoke to her sister on the phone daily, as well as her mother my grandmother. They would talk three, four, five times of day gossiping about what's going in each other's home, or about something that took place in church. My mom is highly intelligent. Prior to having me, she was nurse got her real estate license, and she worked for Copper Craft. After I came along, she became a nurse. I remember her working for a little while, while I was in middle school, but it wasn't long. My mom was stern, she didn't budge much, and she oversaw the house.

My dad went along with just about everything she said. He really didn't have a backbone, I didn't fault him for wanting peace in his home, along with my mom was a nagger. At some point, I assume adhering to her concerns was better than the consequences of going against her. My mom liked to be in control, manipulate, and have the last say. While attending Hubbard Middle School I started observing something about myself. I seemed to have an attraction for women. There was a lady at a church we attended for a while. I always found myself staring at her and her breast I could see these two small balls pointing out her shirt. While she was in the choir stand singing, I was wondering what they were. I used to call her sometimes too, don't even ask me why, because I don't remember. But I do remember asking her what those balls were. She explained they were nipples and helped me to understand what breast were for. Later I found myself being attracted to my female teachers in the seventh and eighth grade.

One teacher was my English Teacher. It was something about her; she was light- skinned, tall, thin; had long black hair, and she drove a white two door Porsche trimmed in black. She was married with two young adult children a boy and girl. I would visit her house sometimes to help her clean. The second teacher was my Global Studies Teacher. My attraction to her was different. She reminded me of my mother, a Deaconess in church, not the same church we attended. Stern and strict, the woman didn't take mess from anybody in our class. If you were talking or misbehaving, she would just lower her glasses on her nose, and say "Do I need to call home?". The difference between her and my mom was I could speak freely with her. I would always stop by her class before going home to say good night.

I remember before graduating the eighth grade and leaving Hubbard Middle School same routine as in the seventh grade she and I had a conversation. She suggested to me that I was gay. I of course denied it, but I did think about what she said to me. She didn't dispute my response to her, she just looked at me, and we changed the conversation. I will admit I didn't like the suggestion and felt that I had to prove her wrong. I didn't know what being gay was, and the only person I knew was gay was my music teacher. I so loved him, he was openly gay, commuted from New York daily, a sharp dresser, and all the female teachers loved him because they were fag hags. Back when I was growing up fag hags were women who loved hanging around gay men. In the back of my head, I was thinking it would explain the attraction I had for my English Teacher. I kept the thought in the back of my mind and made it my life's mission at the time to prove her wrong.

Chapter 2
Church Announcements

As I started high school at Plainfield High, I started to view my mom differently. The older I became the stricter she became. I learned to fear my mom more so than to love my mom. I hated to ask her if I could go somewhere. You see in high school; I made a few friends whom I'm still in touch with today. My friends were always going out on the weekends. They would meet up at each other's houses, have house parties, just having fun.

I could know something for weeks and wait until the last minute to ask out of fear. Fear would overtake me up into the second because now I needed to know the answer. Most of the time the answer was no. My parents were overprotective. It wasn't often, but every now and then she would agree. If I wanted to hang out with my friends, I would have to cut school. We had three cut houses. I helped supply food to the favorite cut house. See, I use to work at the A&P as a cashier. So, whenever my friend's mom would come grocery shopping, I would hook her up not to mention assisting her with getting the crew's favorite foods. The next cut house wasn't really a cut house, it was more our chill house because her parents, and nephew would be home. I loved her house it was always warm an inviting. The last cut house was my boyfriend's house. He had several siblings, so everybody was up in that house. My time at one of the houses was my way of being free. Thinking back, I think they helped me to keep my sanity. Now I really didn't cut class that often to hang with them, because I knew the importance of school, they all lived a distance from my house, and lastly, I lived two blocks from my high school so I had to be home exactly at 3:00 pm or I would get in trouble. One time on my way home I dropped my house keys. I didn't realize it until I got to the front door. Thankfully, the door was open. About thirty minutes later my neighbor came and brought my keys. She gave them to my dad who answered the door. My mother yelled and drilled me about someone could break in our house, and she asked why I didn't go look for my keys when I noticed they were lost. I gave my usually answer "I don't know". But the truth is I really did know, I was scared I was going to be late, and get in trouble. The only day I came home past 3:00pm was on Thursdays because I participated in a after school activity, the Gospel Choir. If we didn't attend our parents were called, and if we stayed later than expected a notice had already been sent home because a show was coming up, or we had to sing somewhere. Signing in the Gospel choir was my other outlet.

I love to sing, and I have a love for music. I sang in the church choir as well. Every third Sunday was Youth Sunday, as most black churches were back in the day. At our church it was customary for all the choirs to march into the church service. I used to love to march in, I thought I was cute back then. Sometimes I would be the lead on a few songs, read scriptures, and pray when asked. Back then I used to love going to church. Zion Hill was a big church, and known all over Newark, NJ. I liked the people there and was fascinated by a few of the women there.

I called one on a regular basis, she was like a mentor to me, but she was fine as hell, and a dope dresser. I'm starting to question the reasons I attended church. Was it for the sex before going to church, or the women I fantasied that attended the church? You see on Sunday's my mom made me attend Sunday School. I didn't mind because after I got my driver's license my dad would let me drive his car and I'd stop past my boyfriend Tyrone's house prior to going to church and get my groove on. In addition, I snuck over to his house the day before going grocery shopping for my mom which she sent me to do every Saturday. We would get it in, then I'd leave to shop at Pathmark around the corner from his house. Every week my mom would ask; What took you so long? and I would be like them lines was long. You know it's the first of the month, I would always have an answer.

Now I know it looks like I was doing all the sneaking. But that wasn't the case. We lived in a bi-level house. so, as I had got older, I moved to the bedroom downstairs for more privacy. I had a living area downstairs, sofa, big floor TV with a balcony door. Tyrone would sneak over around 9p.m. about the time my mom would go to bed. We would be getting in, this night I guess my mom caught on to the adulterated actions in her house and came downstairs and caught us. She beat us both with the vacuum handle. This was the second time we got caught. The first time was when my parents were going to Newark to take care of business. Tyrone came over, we were in my bedroom which at this time was on the main floor next to my mom's room. My parents forgot something and had come back home. We were butt naked. I hid him in my closet and threw some clothes on. I don't know what made my mom come in my room and open the door, but there he was sitting on the floor, he couldn't't hide because he is so dam tall. My mom looked at him, then me, and said get up, put your clothes on and get out of the bedroom. My parents loved him, so he wasn't made to leave the house. We just went somewhere else and got it in. We also got caught a couple of times by Tyrone's dad. His dad saw the perverted version. He would walk in the bedroom, my legs be up in the air, he would stop, look at us because we would stop look at him, he'd walk out shaking his head, and we would continue.

Sometimes on Sundays my stop at his house was a legit stop for he would attend church with me, and we would get it in the car. My dad would say to me "if my cars could talk, they would have a story to tell" he wasn't lying, I knew what time my parents left for church, I had it timed perfectly to be able to get to church before them, participate in the last few minutes of Sunday School to say I attended. I believe this is how I learned to speed which is how I have so many points on my driver's license. Don't get me wrong I knew and loved God, but my intentions were probably impure. I can definitively tell you why I stopped attending church.

At times I was required to see if the Pastor had special announcements needed to be made on Youth Sunday. I would go into the Pastors office and speak with him. He was quite flirtatious, but it didn't bother me. He would always ask me about school, grades, you know the usual small talk adults make for simple conversation. We would discuss some of the other young ladies in the choir that could be my role model. One Sunday in particular, I went into his office, he told me to close the door. I did, he made his usual small talk with me, and preceded to come from behind his chair, and pinned me in the corner. He started kissing me, and put my hands on his penis, he became excited, and became hard. He started feeling on my breast; I couldn't move, lastly, he fingered me. When he was finished, he told me not to tell my parent's and that he couldn't't do this to the girls he suggested to be my role models because of who their parents were in the church. I was sick to my stomach after this day It took years for me to look at church the same, or to trust God. I grew up believing preachers are called by God, so how could this man do this to me, a young adult with no shame. In my eyes he was no different than a sinner off the street. I remember crying at night, just thinking the nastiness of his touch, and his tongue in my mouth, even the thought of his penis. No joke, back then a penis was my best friend; his was repulsive. To this day I never told my parents. My mother felt the pastor could do no wrong, and believed he was the "Truth". Not to long after this incident, I loss interest with singing in the choir, and participating in Youth Sunday. Going to church was a requirement. If you were black and lived in your parent's house who attended church, you were required to go unless you had a great reason. I had the best reason of all, but it was my secret to keep. I shared this secret with one person who I trusted with my life my Tyrone. Prior to saying anything to him after the incident happened, he was sworn to secrecy. He was MAD!!!!!!, I remember he wanted to kill him, I talked him out of it, and he was there for me, and always felt he needed to protect me thereafter, beyond our relationship. I'm just now realizing he was not just my first, but he was my best friend. None of my exes understood our relationship, and until now I don't think I did either. He had witnessed some storms and knew my intimate secrets. Two of those secrets are he was the father of two of my children. I first became pregnant in high school in the eleventh grade. I had an abortion. One of my crushes from my earlier years, who was gay, and his best friend drove us to the clinic in Cherry Hill. After the procedure he took us back to my baby daddy's house. Aside from the two who took us knowing, his dad knew because he paid for it. I remember having to be home by 3:00 so I had to take the bus home form his house. I was in so much pain, just wanted to crawl up in a fetal position, in my bed.

I wish I could say this incident slowed us down, but it didn't, we were back at it three weeks later. We were blessed though because I didn't get pregnant again until our sophomore year in college. I knew I was carrying a girl; she gave me a hell, unlike my first pregnancy which I believed was a boy. I always wanted a boy, and wanted to have Jr. behind his name, so much that when I became older, I didn't call my dad, dad, I called him Jr.

With this pregnancy, I had morning sickness, I ate soup which made my mom suspicious because I hate soup. My number one meal with her was an egg and hamburger sandwich, it was the only meal I didn't bring back up. I thought long and hard about keeping her, but I didn't want to embarrass my family, more so my mother who lived up to the image that we were the perfect family, and I did as well. However, deep in my heart I believe my father knew. After I moved out the house and would come to visit on Sunday's, on this visit he said something to me alluding to he knew I had the abortions. He said, "I know and understand".

Tyrone and I were together about 4 years, but I still had this attraction to females. It was in high school that I met a diverse group of peers, along with teachers. You already know I had crushes on a few teachers, one being my gym teacher who

I called regularly attending while high school and after I graduated. The second, being the school psychologist who was a member of Delta Sigma Theta Sorority Inc. and pinned me when I crossed over, but not any students. I would make sure I visited my now soror every week. Now that I'm thinking about it, I think I was receiving services and didn't even know it. I would have several sessions with her. One of my sessions was a drawing session. From the picture I drew, she identified me as being bi-sexual. I don't know what she asked me to draw, but I was shocked she assessed me as being bi-sexual. After her assessment, I thought back to what my eighth grade Social Studies said about me being gay.

I will say she never changed towards me, as well as my visits with her stayed consistent until she went out on sick leave. None of my high school friends had an inkling of my concerns with my sexual preference not even Tyrone who was getting it in with me on a regular had a clue. I kept everything a secret for fear of my parents finding out. We all know in the age where I grew up being gay was the biggest sin you could commit, because church presented it as if it was the only sin recognized by God. It was safer for me to keep this curiosity to myself and figure it out in the future.   It never left the forefront of my mind. Besides, I had a lot to lose if someone were to find out my secret. One being Tyrone my high school sweetheart. Everybody wanted him, he wasn't the average dude. His attire was not sweatpants, and sneakers. He wore slacks, dress shirts with ties, and dress shoes every day. He was popular, stood 6"2 tall, dark skinned and dressed fly as hell. See he wasn't the average joe who wore jeans, and if he did, he looked ridiculous. You don't know what I had to go through to get him out of the arms of his ex-girlfriend, who until this day, I don't like. She was light skinned, wore glasses, long hair, skinny, and I didn't like her. Let's be clear, she had never done anything to me, I just didn't feel she was the type of young lady he needed. She was too nice and went along with ever he said to do. Not that he was trying to harm her or anything like that. You see, in my head I felt he needed someone bossy, controlling and smothering, not sweet and caring like she was. While dating me Tyrone had no room to breathe, I even had a problem with drawers he would wear. He would like to wear boxers. I was like nah, you got to wear briefs, because I didn't want them chicks to see how big he was when his penis came out his underwear in boxers. He would always say, he needs room for it to breath. I was like you good. When I called, and he wasn't at his house, I would call over to his best friend's house, if his line was busy, I would call the house phone looking for this boy. I believe controlling him was my way of showing him love, whereas he showed me love with kindness, and patience, and I felt his love. I know recognized I was exhibiting characteristics of my mother.

Tyrone and I attended different colleges in different states. I did, however, get accepted to the same college as he, but decided that wasn't a good idea. I attended Stockton State College at the time. After graduating high school, I wanted to be far from home as possible. I loved this college and the freedom I had here. No rules, no curfews. I could breathe. My parents made me come home every weekend, I hated coming home unless, I knew my high school sweetheart was coming home as well, which wasn't 'often. My mother would tell people they had to come get me every weekend because I missed home. This was far from the truth. I hated coming home and didn't want to see them every weekend, but out fear I went along with the facade and not to mention they got tired of coming to get me every weekend. My dad co-signed for me to get a new car. Getting a brand-new car sweetened the deal of having to come home every weekend. One weekend I came home, and my mom and I got into an argument. I don't remember the particulars, but I do remember my dad escorting me to the door and telling me to leave. I would love to say I didn't care, but he hurt my feelings. Maybe because it was my dad who was throwing me out. This was not the last time I was kicked out of the house.

Tyrone and I spoke regularly on the phone with each other. I remember the conversation he and I had like it was yesterday. While discussing how he was trying to get up the money for the abortion, he informed me he was becoming engaged to someone else and wanted his engagement ring back. I was heartbroken because he informed me of this information while pregnant and had the gall to ask for the ring back for some chick in the south where he attended college. I wasn't hurt that he was seeing someone else, because I had my own secrets I was trying to come to terms with, but to ask while pregnant with his child, having morning sickness, crazy cravings, and his concern was getting engaged. In addition, too he was still searching for the funds for the abortion.

Well, his daddy who was like a dad to me came through for us again, he came up with money, and my best friend in college, Elisha, took me to get the abortion in Atlantic City. I remember Elisha dropping me off at home, and I went right to bed from all the pain I was in. Although Elisha and Tyrone checked on me, I felt so alone. After, I got myself together I told a friend about the nerve of him asking for his ring to give to some other chick. They suggested I pawn the engagement ring, and that's what I did. I can't remember the amount I received for it, but I remember going shopping. After the pregnancy, and the pawning of the ring we became distance for a short while.

Upon coming home for summer break from college, I started working at the YMCA as a Youth Counselor, in Plainfield NJ. Tyrone and I started speaking again. Whenever he had something to do and couldn't use his dad's car, he would drop me off at work and take my car. One morning we were parked outside the YMCA, I was talking, not sure what about, but I know it wasn't about our relationship because were no longer involved with a title but were still getting our groove on. During this conversation I just bust out screaming, and crying, I was having a nervous breakdown. He didn't know how to react, he was listening and understood because he had experienced firsthand how mean, and strict my mom was. He knew a lot about my home life, and I how felt about my parents, and how I was treated. One Sunday just before Tyrone left to go home, we were having a family discussion, I'm not sure of the topic. All I know, I saw him out, and he pulled off. I returned upstairs to the kitchen and was standing at the kitchen sink washing dishes. My mom came from behind me told me to turn around and she slapped the mess out of me. She stated, "don't be telling our family business." To this day I don't know why she slapped me, and I never asked, it was also the last time she hit me. That slap has been an unpleasant memory all these years.
Don't get me wrong, I wasn't physically abused, but I believe I was emotionally abused. My mom would just say things which

hurt me, and because I feared her, I would never defend myself, and this did not change upon me becoming an adult. All this bottled-up emotion was released in rage while we sat in the car in front of my job. He held me we discussed my melt down before I went inside to work. I couldn't have been in a safer space at that moment in time. I felt the weight of the world lifted off my shoulders. He always had my back as my boyfriend and is loyal friend. This is another secret under his belt which he has kept about me.

Working at the YMCA is the start to me working with children. I worked there for about three years. I was assigned children whose ages ranged six-eight years of age. I enjoyed working with these young people. I was younger, in college and exhibited more patience. What I remember most about this job, and carry with me until now, was a short, light skinned, curly haired, cute as a button, little boy whom I was assisting with his homework and, I observed the young man could not read. I would categorize the book he was reading like the "Cat in a The Hat" book. The young man could read certain words and learned to memorized different words because of the pictures. This was a major concern for me. It really bothered me that as young as he was none of his teachers, or parents knew this baby was faking knowing how to read. I reported this to my supervisor at the time who happened to be a retired schoolteacher, who assigned someone to get this child the help he needed. I believe this is the job that opened my awareness for the love of working with children.

At the end of summer break, I returned to Stockton where I resided off campus with three young ladies, and two gentlemen who were brothers to one of the young ladies. We became roommates at the end of my freshman year of college where we lived in Absecon, NJ then we moved to Oakcrest Estates in Mays Landing, NJ in a townhouse. This is where I fell in love with townhouses. To support myself, I worked part time at the Tropicana Resort & Hotel in room service. One evening, I got called into work. It was a slow night because it was snowing. There was a bartender there who worked in the same department who liked one of my roommates. He asked me did I want an Iced Tea, and I don't mean sweet tea. I replied sure. Honey, till this day I will not drink an Iced Tea. That drink was strong as hell. My head was spinning, I kept puking, they had to send me home; but don't worry they didn't know I was drunk. I enjoyed this job, I had some good times, with good tips.

Being independent at Stockton was good for me, I was dating a young guy who was pledging Iota Theta. He was on line, and I would sneak to see him. This night I was not the only one who came to see him, his big brothers came barging in and he along with his roommate who was also on line shoved me under the bed. Mind you I was much skinner then to fit. This is where I also learned about the Divine 9, their parties, and let's not forget to mention about the house parties. These kids today don't know nothing about house parties, the drinks, and clean fun.

Stockton will always be special to me. It was the location where I decided to answer the questions I needed to know about my sexuality. My surrounding's there were different. Having been sheltered for years, this was a new exciting experience. I was now exposed to a diverse set of lifestyles. I was fascinated by what I saw, and who I met. I dated a few guys while attending Stockton; a few were on campus and one special one off campus. The dudes I dated on campus were really booty calls, nothing serious, nor satisfying. Mentally I was in a place of trying to prove I was straight to myself because no one knew that I was questioning who I was. In addition, too I was addicted to sex. If I must come to terms with my demons, I was a ho, seeking love, acceptance, who just wanted to have an orgasm. Being young and naïve, searching for me with guys who probably didn't know my name. Their only concern was having an orgasm and moving on to the next thing.

I did however, meet a young man who didn't attend Stockton, but lived in the area. He was a musician who played for the Stockton Gospel Choir which I sung in. Bubbles was about my height and chunky, but a true sweetheart, horrible in bed, but treated me well. When I wasn't in class, I spent most of time at his house. His dad was a pastor, and his mom was sweet as pie, cooked her behind off, and truly was a child of God. On Sundays I attended church with his family. I so loved his entire family. We weren't together when his mom passed, out of respect for how she treated me and made me feel so welcomed in her home, I did attend the service.

There was something about this boy; I don't know what because I like my men slim and tall, not short and chunky. It appears we were always together. When the choir had singing engagements, I didn't ride on the bus with the choir; he came and picked me up until he got kicked off campus for fighting. Which worked out for me because he would let me borrow his car. During this time, I still lived in the campus apartments. It was through him I met different types of people. What I mean by this is his friends were into church; their singing groups performed and played for various church choirs and were members of his dad's church.

Bubbles was also friends with a criminal named Ralph who has since changed his ways. Ralph's parents were professionals; a teacher and police officer who were highly respected in the community. I enjoyed hanging with them, it was through all this activity I was starting to slowly believe in God again after being molested. When I wasn't with Bubbles or my roommates during this time on campus and I would hang out at Ralph's house. One of my roommates was dating Ralph, and this was our new hangout. All this hanging out was exciting to me. My roommate who was dating Ralph was also from Plainfield. She was also dating a dude in Plainfield, and sometimes in the middle of the night my room mates and I would ride with her to visit him. We weren't too far from my house, but I wouldn't dare inform my parents I was in the area for fear of all the questions, and then they might start monitoring my activities. In my eyes, I was grown and doing me until the weekend when they would come to pick me up. I'm not sure of the reason Bubbles and I broke up. I do remember however, being intimate with Bubbles always meant me being on top. It wasn't that he was terrible in bed, I was still a sex addict, and would have to have an orgasm. The problem with him was he couldn't work it from the top, so I worked him from the top, and this is how I would have an orgasm. Now mind you, when I would visit home on the weekends, and Tyrone came home from college to visit, we were still getting it in. This is how I got pregnant while I was in college, and probably the reason why Bubbles and I broke up. Bubbles didn't know I was pregnant or sleeping with someone else. I guess my morals kicked in, and we ended the relationship. While still pregnant with Tyrone's child, I went to the mall in Atlantic City, and saw this young woman who caught my eye. I walked near the booth where she was working. You know how we have the store set up in the middle of the mall outside the actual stores. I walked over to her to look like I was interested in the items the store sold. But really, I was looking at my new item of interest; her.

After my abortion, my focus is back on me and my truth. I found myself visiting the mall often because she had my attention. She was about my height, a couple of years older than me, nice caramel skin, short curly hair, her swag was an athletic walk, nice dresser, beautiful smile, and I loved her lips. This is all new for me. I've never approached a woman before, let alone told a female I'm attracted to her. I didn't know what to say. I didn't even know if she was gay. As we called it back in the day, my gay radar was/is not perfected. I was just going on how she dressed, walked, more importantly, my attraction to this chick. After several visits to the mall walking around her area, she noticed me. We started talking with small talk, like where I was from, where I attended college, where was I living off campus. Her name was Charlotte, she lived in the area, and this was her part time job. I left the mall with those digits, and a smile on my face. Now, what the hell am I going to do with these digits, and what the hell was I gonna say; were my first panicked thoughts. I had to be smooth with it, not looking desperate trying to figure out who I was, as well, as walking into a lifestyle I knew nothing about. I called Charlotte. She was single at the time, and we started hanging out at her house. We would grab a bite to eat, and let's not forget where it all started, I would visit with her at work. I told her the truth about my attraction to her, and she is the first woman, admitted this too. One evening I went over to her house we were horse playing around, watching television. It was getting late, and time for me to leave, but before I left, I got my nerve up to kiss her. I don't mean I peck on the lips either, it was a long tongue kiss, then I left. On my drive home all I could think about was this kiss, and that this kiss was with a woman. Now, who could I tell? Yes! There was someone I could tell my friend Elisha. Elisha is a private person, not many people knew she was gay. She and I clicked as soon as we met, not to mention she took me to get my second abortion. I called her right away and informed her about the encounter, she was shocked and wanted to know all the details which I filled her in. After experiencing my first kiss, Elisha became like a mentor to me. She schooled me on how women like to be touched with a softness, and when caressing and sucking a women's breast be gentle.

Nothing ever became of my relationship with Charlotte, I will always have love in my heart for her because she helped with me taking the first step. I needed to identify myself. We remained good friends for many years long after I left Stockton.

Chapter 3
Living in Confusion

That kiss was a start to a whole new life, and not in a good way. The semester was ending, my grades had dropped, my mother must have sensed something was going on because she called and informed me if I wanted her to continue paying for my education I had to come home. This was the worst news ever, I was enjoying my life, finally fitting in with real friends, didn't have to answer to anyone, and most importantly, I was starting to identify my sexuality. I remember my parents pulling up packing up the car, and me not wanting to leave, but had no choice.

I attended Kean College for summer classes and was accepted into Jersey City State College in the fall. At first, I didn't jell with Jersey City. It seemed I couldn't find the gay people. I met this guy named John he was built like Shaq and played basketball for the college. He was housed on campus where I spent a lot of my time in between watching the college basketball games. He became my new man and something to do since my life was starting over. I remember me and him this big bear, both trying to fit in his twin bed. This was not a comfortable nor a cute picture, but he made it work when it became necessary. If I wasn't spending time with him, I was participating in the gospel choir. As with most choirs we attended several engagements. So, I was able to get out of the house, with a valid excuse. My parents had me on a 12:00am curfew. What fun could I have before 12:00 am? Your correct, NONE! Now mind you, when I was in high school, my curfew was 12:00am. That time did change three times, one being for prom. I had to be home at 1:00 am. My parents agreed to this timeline because they knew the schedule for the prom. However, we left the prom early to get something to eat. We ended up at White Castles, our favorite spot. We saw one of my mom's friends from church there. She complimented us on how we looked and asked where we were coming from. We explained the occasion, and again she complimented us. As the tradition still stands everyone goes to Great Adventure after the prom. I thought I was going too, until my mom's friend whom we had seen at White Castle's earlier in the morning decided to call my mom and tell her she saw us, and where she saw us at. I got in trouble for not calling home and telling my parents where we decided to go before, I returned home. Well, because of these events of the big mouth friend, I was not allowed to go. I was really upset that I was missing out on the fun, and felt my parents were mean as hell, and wrong for this. The next time I was allowed a late night was leading up to my college graduation. A graduation event was taking place on a boat at the harbor in Jersey City. The graduation class of 91 was sponsoring a boat ride for graduation. I took a guest for the event. I was scheduled to take my sands. Instead, I took this chick I met at the Greek store in Plainfield. I would go in the store occasionally, try and get my mac on and she seemed interested; but thinking back, I'm not sure if she was gay, straight or bi-sexual. She was thin, light skin, with curly hair, and never smiled. I had the worse time ever I was ready to go home before my curfew. I told my sands I was bored as hell. She told me that's what I get for taken the chick and cancelling with her. She ain't never lied. These were the two exemptions of extending my curfew. Now we all know that's when black folks leave the house to go to the party.

Lastly, while attending Jersey City State College I attended a Rush for Delta Sigma Theta Sorority INC. This is an event I will never forget. The Rush was held at Rutgers University, the room was crowded with young ladies who attended several different colleges from the North Jersey surrounding areas anxious to pledge Delta Sigma Theta INC. The Sorors asked a question: "Give one word that describes you". They went around the room for each young lady to answer. My answer to the question was Determination. I live by this word until today. When people tell me I can't accomplish something, I make it my mission to prove them wrong. I'm determined to have the best in life with God's help and favored blessings.

After the rush, we had to approach the Delta Sigma Theta INC. women at the table and pick up the applications on the way out. Being that I'm newly transferred into Jersey City State, and my credits were coming from Stockton, Kean, and Jersey City State, I asked was I able to apply. The young lady informed me no and stated to try again next year. Her answer did not sit well with me. I took the application, gathered my letters of recommendation, called a member of my church who was a soror and a member of the chapter who oversees the Intake Process, I explained to her what I was told, and she advised me to still apply, which were my sentiments exactly. And so, I did, along with Kelly whom I met at the rush who attended the same college as I. We became cool and started hanging together. When people saw me, they saw her. We formed a bond while waiting to get the phone call with a date, and time for an interview. Anyone who has pledged has experienced this feeling. A week might have gone by, and yes,

I received a call with the information. Of course, I called Kelly
to find out if she received a call, and she stated she had; our
appointments were on different days and was I nervous as hell.
I had to pick out a dressy outfit, couldn't wear the
organizations colors, not even a hint. Kelly and I studied
everything we thought we needed to know for our interview.
If you have the pleasure of being a part of the Divine 9 you
know the nervous feeling you get arriving to the interview, let
alone walking to interview for something you have longed to
be a part of.

   After my interview, I was anxious to know if they chose
me. It seemed like forever, waiting to find out the
results. Days went buy, working, going to class, not paying
attention. Calling Kelly to find if she "got the call". She was just
as anxious as I was. I remember being home on a Thursday
evening, not to long after getting home from work, doing
homework. Around 9:00pm I GOT THE CALL! I was so happy I
called Kelly; she got the call as well. She and I were screaming.
We were so happy, my mom wanted to know what was going
on.
I told her Delta Sigma Theta Sorority Called and I was chosen
for membership intake. Weeks went by, attending classes,
trying to do homework, going to work when I could, coming
home all times of night, until my twenty-six Sands and I
crossed over December 7th, 1991, at Rutgers New Brunswick.
The first place we headed was to the Greek Shop in East
Orange, New Jersey. Montclair State was having a party, and
us Neo's had to take it over. I'm officially a Delta, withholding
my sexual preference. Out of twenty-six sands I put my trust in
two Sands to divulge my secret to. One being Pamaline who

is also my baby's momma, her two children are my Godchildren. Pamaline and I were driving to one of the colleges to visit our sands one day. While I was driving, I remember telling Pamaline I have an attraction to women. She said, "Do you like me" I said no, she replied, "I don't give a fuck then." From that day to this, that's my bestie.

I continued with Sociology as my major, and in one of my Sociology classes attended a mature woman whose name was Barbara, who loved God and was cool as hell. We were paired up to complete a project. I forget what the assignment was, but it led us to New York City. This was my first time in the Big Apple, I was so excited, and fascinated by the large buildings the train, and the crowd of people. We met at a shop in New York, it was there I felt comfortable enough to explain my confusion to her. Although, she was religious her advice was not telling me it's a sin to be gay and pray to God and ask him to remove the sin. On the contrary, she advised me to pray and seek God to answer the question that would remove my doubts, and confusion. In addition, to this, it just so happened she had a friend who was gay and lived in Jersey City. She said she would pass my number along.

After completing our project, we walked around New York City. I was in awe of the crowd, the diverse people, and we saw a lot of gay clubs. She suggested that I might visit one. I looked at her and said I'm not going by myself. Although it was a good idea who was I going to get to go with me? Now Pamaline was not comfortable enough to hang out with other gay people. So that leads me to another one of my sands whose personality was more accepting. More accepting in the sense of accompanying me to a gay club, to help me experience gay life. I had an honest conversation with Nando explaining my confusion, lack of experience, and more importantly, my struggle with believing in God, and being gay. Growing up in my era all the church spoke of was homosexuality is a sin. It had me really thinking that was the only sin in the Bible. It seemed like if you identified as being gay in the black community you were labeled the "black sheep" of the family. Speaking with Nando was like having therapy, she had a lot of wisdom. Her advice was I couldn't keep hiding who I was, living in confusion, and not knowing where I fit in life. She also explained my belief in God would direct me to being happy whether straight or gay.

After this conversation, I asked Nando to accompany me to a gay club in New York, she agreed. I must admit I did have a little bit of a crush on Nando, but I never disrespected her.

I found a club that I was interested in, and we ventured to my first gay club on Christopher Street in New York. We walked into the gay world, people dancing, kissing, relaxing, and having fun. Upon arriving we lucked up to find a table and were seated. We met a few people who asked Nando to dance. She first explained she was not gay, and she was there for support then she proceeded to dance. I tell you she had more fun than I did, not to mention I don't like to dance because I don't know how; I have no rhythm. Although, I enjoyed myself, and experienced a new world and lifestyle I wasn't quite comfortable returning to New York by myself to go clubbing just yet.

The weekend was over and I was back in class, and I'm telling my friend Barbara about my exciting weekend in New

York. She had exciting news for me as well. She told her friend about me, and she wanted to meet up. I was so excited, but nervous as well. Aside from spending time with Charlotte which resulted in my first kiss, I hadn't any experience with women. Some days went by, before I received the phone call from Wanna. She and I had great conversation on the phone not to mention she had a sexy voice and was a few years older than me. We spoke regularly, and I was honest about having not been with women and could possibly be bi-sexual because I was still sleeping with Tyrone. After several conversations we agreed to meet up. Wanna lived in Jersey City not too far from the college, so she invited me over to her house. I was nervous, but excited to meet her in person.

I arrived at her home, rang the doorbell, she took a few minutes to answer, then came to the door. There she stood about my height 5'6, dark skinned, thick, but not fat, short haircut, dark lips because she smoked, an attractive young lady. Wanna's mom, and sister were home as well. We chilled in her bedroom talked and watched television. There was a mutual attraction, with one problem. Wanna was in a relationship. I respected this and she and I grew to be close friends. We still hung out, but my attraction to her did not change.

Now that I had added another friend in my life, my answer to whether I'm gay or not was still in question. Wanna and I were talking one evening, and she said, "I'm going to find you a girlfriend". I replied "Ok". She knew of someone that also attended Stockton and had returned home. She said she would give her a call and see what's up. Come to find out old girl was single and wanted to meet up. We were now in the month of July no further knowing if I was gay or not than I was in January. Before meeting up, we exchanged numbers, and were talking on the phone regularly, we had a lot of things in common. Having returned home from Stockton, and being older than me, she didn't want to live with her grandmother. She was staying with a male friend and his family who lived in Newark, NJ until she was able to get own her apartment. She also hung out in East Orange with her friends. We initially met up at her friend's house in East Orange. I immediately recognized her from Stockton, she was no stranger to me. I remember she and her girlfriend at the time were always together in school; they were inseparable. Jazmin was my height as well, a femme, prissy, dark skin, long hair, and petite. She recognized me as well. We were comfortable with each other, on days I had classes I would stop in East Orange to chill and spend time with her and her friends.

Well, towards the end of July, my parents, had a trip planned with my aunt and uncle to go down South to a family reunion. They were trying to convince me to take the trip with them. Oh, hell naw!!! I can't stand the south, I don't like going down south, nor do I like the people in the South. Not to mention why would I go with them and miss being home by myself with no one to answer to. How crazy do I look!!!? Now mind you, even though I wasn't going with them that didn't stop me from getting all the details such as when ya'll leaving, what time ya'll leaving, and when ya'll coming back. While they were planning, I was planning my own thing with Jazmin. I asked her was she free that weekend, and she was. Finally, the weekend has arrived. My family left for the family reunion. I'm all excited, cleaning up the house, getting myself together before she came over. I'm nervous as hell, because I don't know what to expect, how to act, or what to do when she comes arrived.

She arrived around 10:00 in the morning, I opened the door she has on a see-through pink, short sleeve top, and a pair of white shorts. She came downstairs to my section of the house. We were sitting on the sofa chilling. She asked me was I hungry, I said yea, she asked what I wanted to eat. I was like grits, eggs, and bacon. She stood up, took her shirt, and bra off. And went upstairs to the kitchen and cooked. Now mind you I still haven't slept with a female yet, but I was excited as hell, not to mention I was just staring at her. I must say the girl could cook, but breakfast is no longer my focus.

After she fed me breakfast, we cleaned the kitchen and went back downstairs to the sofa. My back was to the end of the sofa, and she's sitting between my legs. We started kissing and my hands were feeling her breast. I flipped her, and started sucking her breast, and the rest is history. Afterwards, she left, we were to meet up later with Wanna and some of her friends and go to Brooklyn NY.

I was sitting downstairs smiling, reminiscing about my experience with a female, and how it felt so natural to be with a female when my doorbell rang. I was like who the hell at my door? I looked out the window and it was my cousin's husband Roland's car. Now I was thinking what the hell does he want.

I opened the door and let him in and went downstairs to my quarters. He's likes hey, wanted to check on you while the family was away. I told him I'm good, and that I had plans for the night. I went in my bedroom to get something, and he followed me in the room. He pushed me down on the bed and held me down. He was trying to tongue kiss me; I was moving turning my face to keep him from succeeding. He was holding me down, I was moving as much as I could to try and get away from him, but he was stronger than I. He pulled my shorts down and began to rape me. When he was finished, he got up and left. I didn't know what to do, who to tell, how to feel. I went and took a shower. I couldn't get his smell off me for months. My day had become traumatic, I don't know what I should be doing. I was staring at the clock, knowing the best part of my day, the answer to my question about my sexuality had now been ruined, and I had plans to meet up with the chick who helped answer this question.

It took me a while before I got myself together, meaning my thoughts, thinking about his scent embedded in my nose, and on my body. I didn't want to be in the house by myself, nor did I want to lay in the bed where he raped me, so I got myself together went to East Orange to meet Jazmin. I arrived there to see her and wanted to smile, but couldn't, I knew I was distant towards her, but I also wanted to forget how Roland, my cousin's husband, had raped me. I got in the car with Jazmin, and we headed to Union Station in Newark, NJ to catch the train to Brooklyn, NY where we met up with Wanna her girlfriend, and a few of her friends.
Although the rape took place being around people kept my mind off the incident. The females I met in New York, were nice people, along with Wanna's girlfriend who was attractive and pleasant. I could tell she was really into Wanna. Not to mention Wanna's friends were the best host and made me feel at home. Something I needed at this point after being violated in my home. They cooked us dinner, we played some games while listening to music.

While I was in New York my mom called. I had to step away so she wouldn't ask additional questions about the background noise. She asked how I was doing and was everything alright at home. I replied yes, she further stated my cousins have been calling me, to check up on me, and wanted me to come to Sunday dinner, but couldn't get a hold of me. I told my mom, I was good, and had been eating so I didn't need to go to their house for dinner. Not to mention, I was happy where I was in New York, and had no need to be under the same roof as my rapist. I had such a great time, until it was time for us leave. Part of me wanted to stay in Brooklyn, and not return home, but that was not possible.

I got back home and washed my sheets before getting in my head. I had decided I couldn't tell anyone in my family what happened. Who would they believe me or him? He was my cousin's husband, who would, or could believe he was a rapist, not to mention, rape me who was so much younger than he and related to his wife. The only person I could tell was my faithful secrete keeper Tyrone. Sometime has gone by and I hadn't seen Tyrone to tell him what happened. Although, I was coping, as best I could, I believe I was in denial, as well as adapting to finally recognizing I'm a lesbian.

Jazmin and I are hanging out a lot in the bedroom. Outside of the bedroom I was learning more about Jazmin such as she was homeless, bi- sexual, did not have a job, was toying with the guy she lives with, and had a urinary tract infection, not to mention she couldn't pay her cell bill and now she was asking me for money. I can't help you sista. Jazmine was an opportunist and was not the woman for me. Her cell phone got cut off, and our only way of communicating was her

JUST BEYOND THE BRIDGE

calling collect and me accepting the charges. Me being young and pussy whooped didn't realized how much the phone bill would be. Back then we had the teenage line which was an addition to the main line in the house. CHIIE!!!! when my mother got that phone bill. She went through the roof. She wanted to know who the hell was calling collect, and why did we have to talk so dam much. I looked dumbfounded because you already know I didn't have an answer. But I tried, and said she was having problems and needed someone to talk with. My mother gave me that look, ya'll know the 'I know your ass is lying 'look. I did however, come up with the money to pay the phone bill.

Finally, Jazmine was able to get an efficiency apartment, she became employed, and was starting to get on her feet so I thought. She still wanted help, and I was not in the position to assist her. She had other people to ask like the dude from Newark who was already helping her with her bills, as well as sleeping with her. I must say he was a genuinely nice Christian, naive guy who wasn't aware she liked women, and it was not my place to expose her lies. After all, she and I were just sex buddies. Eventually, I realized who she was and began to step off. I had a conversation with Wanna giving her the 411 about her friend. She apologized, and advised me to move on, which I did. Jazmine didn't care she was already on to the next to help with her bills. As it turns out Wanna was no longer in a relationship. She told me they broke up a couple of weeks ago, in my head I'm like hell yea!!! So, we started kicking it. It was New Year's Day we were over my cousin's house whose husband is my rapist for our annual diner. I really didn't want to go but had no choice because I couldn't tell the truth for my not wanting to go. The good thing was I had plans to be Wanna after we ate dinner. My mom was like where are you going, I replied, over Wanna's house. My mom knew Wanna, she would come over and spend time at my house without my mother ever suspecting she or I was gay. I could tell she really didn't want me to go, but at this point I'm in my early 20's so she had to loosen my collar.

When I arrived at Wanna's, her mom said she was in her room go on. I went in her room she had just got out the shower and was wearing a red robe. She turned around towards me, opened her robe, grabbed me and kissed me. see what I didn't tell you about Wanna is that she smoked. That was a turn on for me. Whenever we had sex, she would have a cigarette, and I would make sure I kissed her when she was finished smoking. She and I went out on dates, hung out in Brooklyn with her friends I met when I was seeing Jazmine. I was really enjoying myself and figuring out this gay thing. Meanwhile, I was still seeing Tyrone when he would come home from college. Wanna knew of my love for Tyrone, and he was always aware of the ladies in my life. He didn't try to change me, he was involved with someone, no pressure, good friends, still good sex. Now Wanna on the other hand, I was in love with this girl, who was not aware I was still kicking it with Tyrone, she and I had no title on our relationship, so I wasn't cheating. She did, however, have a problem with bi-sexual women and wasn't thrilled when I would tell her when I saw or was with Tyrone. The one thing I never did was lie to her nor to him. It came down to she was becoming jealous of Tyrone, so I stepped back from him a little, he was getting ready to return to college soon no biggy.

Soon after he left, she and I broke up. I'm not gonna even lie, I begged for us to get back together. Toward the end of our relationship, she wanted me to buy her a ferret. I was like I don't have money to buy you a ferret.

After we broke up, I was willing to try and find the money to buy this girl a ferret. She was like it's too late. I was devasted over this break up, but I survived. We became close friends to the point I hooked her up with her next girlfriend, and they started a life in Florida together. Everything worked out for the best anyway. My parents sold the house in Plainfield and bought another home in Manahawkin, NJ.

Chapter 4
How Did I Get Here?

We now live in another suburban neighborhood, but this time most of our neighbors are caucasians. The other black people in the neighborhood are my aunt and uncle who lived next door. I hated moving from my roots in Plainfield. There was nothing to do in Manahawkin, nor did I have friends in this area. It was like starting life all over again. I had just found the gay people, and now I lived in no man's land with all these old retired white people, and if they weren't old, they were white married couples with little children.

For a while I drove back and forth to North Jersey because I worked in Elizabeth, NJ as an assistant to my old boss's daughter from when I worked at the YMCA in Plainfield. I filed, answered phones, socialized, no different from what I do now. I liked my job, could have advanced in the company if I had of just gone to the interview. For some reason I got scared and skipped the interview. I already knew the position was mine. Looking back, God had other plans.

I was driving to and from North Jersey daily and got into a car accident. This was a wakeup call, either I move back to North Jersey with Lauren, a classmate from college who lived in an apartment with a spare room for rent or find employment at my new location. I really wanted to move back up north, but fear took over. My curfew was upgraded to 1:00 am if I wasn't working. I did, however, find another job in North Jersey which was part time working in a group home. Sometimes after work I would head over to Murphy's a gay Club in Newark, just to be around the gay crowd. I love to watch the gay men dance to the original "It's Time for the

Peculator". Now if you've ever been to Murphy's, you know it was a small club, standing room only, but it was the best spot to be in next to being in New York. As time went by, I got tired of driving to North Jersey, and I decided to find employment closer to home.

I applied at Covenant House in Atlantic City for the position of a Youth Case Manager. I knew a few people who were also employed there who graduated from Stockton. Covenant House hired me full time for the 4-12pm shift. Through working here, I was meeting different people and starting to make friends. In addition, I was closer to home, so hanging out late was awesome I didn't have to rush home. Now Atlantic City and I were far from strangers. I have plenty of history in A.C. starting with working there while in college, and my first kiss. It was just the matter of picking up where I left off. My friend Elisha still lived in the area so we would meet up from time to time.

One weekend I was invited over to a friend's house for a get together where I met a young lady who was on the soft butch side, pretty skin, had a short haircut with Indian hair, and was a fast talker. We started talking, exchanged numbers, and then started hanging out.

I saw the red flags but ignored them. Don't get me wrong Dinna was good a hearted person, but she was running from the law, and stated she was a recovering cocaine addict. She stayed at the Hi Hoe Hotel on the pike in Atlantic City. I spent a lot of my days in this one room small hotel with Dinna. I would either stop to see her before or after work, and of course we spoke on my breaks at work. Dinna's sister lived in Plainfield, my hometown. Dinna didn't work and because of her legal troubles, she was wanted by the FED's. She did however receive a monthly allowance from her deceased parents 'inheritance. We would drive up to North Jersey to hang out with her sister and pick up the check. I enjoyed visiting her sister she had a huge, beautiful home, she would either take us out to dinner, or she would order food whenever we came up.

Our relationship started to grow, and we had great sex, and I even invited her over for Easter Dinner which was in a couple of weeks. I really wasn't trying to rush into a relationship with her because she could be a fast talker at times, which made me hesitant. During one of our many conversations about our sex life, we were on the phone reminiscing "about last night" that conversation lasted over an hour. A few days later I received a call from my cousin stating her mom, my aunt was listening in on the conversation. I asked how, she said the phone lines crossed and she was listening. Back in the day we had the thick cordless phones, and being that we were next door to each other, the lines crossed. My cousin said my aunt heard the entire conversation and knows I'm gay and intends to tell my mom.

I thanked her for the heads up. I remember the conversation I had with Dinna clear as day, it was a provocative, explicit sexual conversation which should have made a straight person sick to their stomach especially as for as long as the conversation went on.
I was nervous, I knew all hell is about to hit the fan especially since I invited her over for Easter Dinner. I walked around the house on eggshells waiting for the bomb to drop. I became

uncomfortable around my family. I felt as though I was being watched by my aunt who was waiting to drop the bomb. Easter Sunday is quickly approaching, I don't know what to do, tell her not to come, or let all break loose. My travels to work were different now. When I stopped passed Dinna's room, I didn't stay long for fear of being questioned of my whereabouts. I know my family; my aunt had already told my mom.

My mom policed my every movement when I was leaving the house. I knew dinner would not be a pleasant experience for neither of us because I overheard my mom on the phone talking about me bringing Dinna over for dinner. Her and my aunt had plans, which would have resulted in a horrific experience. The story gets worse. Covenant House changed my schedule for that weekend. I was to work a double overnight until 4pm Easter Sunday. For fear of my mother and knowing in my head she was not going to believe my schedule changed I left my shift early, stopped passed Dinna's to tell her I had to uninvite her to dinner because my family has a unpleasant plan for you if you come over, she understood. This was not her first rodeo with being gay and meeting the persons she's dating family. I went home afterwards and acted like I didn't know a thing and ate the traditional Easter dinner with the family.

The next day I returned to work, acting like I didn't leave my shift yesterday. As soon as I walked in, I was called to my supervisor's office. She asked me did I not see the new schedule. I lied and responded no. She didn't believe me, I tried to plead my case still lying though, and was terminated effective immediately. I was so hurt all because of fear that I carried in my own head of my parents knowing I was gay. I got caught up in abandoning my job that was in my degree area of study that paid me well. I left Covenant House and spent the rest of my shift at Dinna's.

I went home as if I was at work all day. I went to my room and was trying to figure out how was I going to explain getting fired, and more importantly, where was I going to find another good paying job. Not too long after being in my room, my mom called me downstairs to the family room. Both my parents were sitting in there then comes my aunt walking through the front door. My mom asked me did I have something to tell them. I said no.

Then my aunt took over the conversation, she spoke of how she overheard my conversation on the phone with that dike, and she rather me be a drug addict than for me to be gay. My mother stated she always knew I was gay
because she noticed boys had stopped coming over to the house.

She went on to say she always told me I could come to talk to her about anything. I just stood there looking at them, like I was crazy. My dad was quiet during my execution, my mother started crying and told me I needed to get out.

I headed out the door went back to Dinna's and told her what happened. She suggested we get an apartment together. Being that I was desperate this seemed to be a great idea. We started looking in the paper for apartments. It was easy for me to get out of the house because my parents didn't know I lost my job, in addition I had one paycheck left which would have made proof of income I had to act fast.

My mother seemed distance toward me and appeared to become spiteful. I remember a phone bill came and she showed me the portion I had to pay which was no higher than usual, she was going off on me about the bill and told me if I could afford to waste my money on a high phone bill that she could increase the amount of rent I was paying. Which she held true to after which the light bulb went off in my head and I caught a clue. For the amount she raised my rent too, I could move out, and not answer to her rules, no curfew and would be ok.

Dinna and I found and were approved for a nice affordable 2-bedroom apartment in Pleasantville with the pool right in front of our door. The apartment was in my name. We had to go to North Jersey monthly to collect Dinna's inheritance money for her share of the rent.
After we signed the lease, I had to tell my parents I was moving. I don't think they thought I would be that quick. They were surprised, and my mother swears she didn't tell me to leave. She was sad to me see my go, but I was out that piece.

While looking for apartments I also was seeking employment. I applied at the Atlantic City Board of Education as a Security Officer; I was notified of my start date at Atlantic City High School not to long after we moved into the apartment. This would be new for me, now that I was living on my own, I had to make wiser decisions. It's my first day at work, Dinna dropped me off and picked me up. We only had the one vehicle so we agreed she would look for under the table work while I was at work. I enjoyed the job; I was able to grab over time hours being Atlantic City High School was just built and needed security around the clock.

Working around the students was a real joy for me. I was able to advise students to further their education by going to college, discuss with them the importance of not cutting their classes, not to mention I didn't want to take them to the office. I often was able to work overtime during the evening which assisted a lot with my share of the bills in the apartment. We were struggling, but it was all good. I worked in the position of a Security Guard for maybe six months before my immediate Supervisor called me in his office and asked me didn't I have a degree. I said yes, and he proceeded to advise me to apply to become a substitute teacher. I took him up on his advice and applied. After receiving my certificate for Atlantic City School District, I applied in the Pleasantville School District as well to give me more options. I resigned working as a Security Guard and started working as a substitute teacher. I worked more in the Pleasantville School District then I did Atlantic City District. When a sub was needed, they would call around 6-6:30am in the morning. The secretary at the time who assigned the subs, liked me and called me every day. I took all the age groups but hated the elementary schools. Little kids were not my thing. As I put my time in, I was able to request working with the high school students. I worked for years in this position to the degree I was forced to pay into the Pension as a substitute.

While it seemed to be upgrading my resume, Dinna was working under the table and using my car still for work. Not only was she working under the table she was working my bank account stealing money.

What made me pay attention to it was I always hid money in the house. I noticed it was missing so I went to the Mac machine to withdraw money and noticed my account was low and asked her about it. She denied taking the money from the account but stated she knew who did. She accused a mutual friend of ours who really was her friend prior to me coming along. I knew she was lying because he didn't have a reason to steal from me because he was our go to guy. He liked Dinna, so when we were short on the bills, he lent us the money until one of us got paid.

As it turns out she was robbing me blind. I started paying close attention to my account and her habits. One weekend she went up North Jersey to stay a few days with her sister. I received a phone call from a dude she hung around. He told me this was a courtesy call because he liked me and didn't want any harm to come to me. Dude continued to say Dinna owes him a lot of money, and he wants his money. He also warned me that while I'm at work she lets him and two of his friends use my car to make his runs. This is how she makes payments when her funds are low. When I heard this, I had to call my friend Elisha to give her the low down, I was furious.

When Dinna returned from her sister's I stopped letting her drive my car. My keys were always in my presence to the point to this day I know the sound of my keys and when my keys move. She didn't know what was going on, then I really noticed her mood swings. She was so desperate she sent me to the dude's house to pick up an envelope. I went, picked it up, chit chatted with dude a few minutes. When I drove off something said look in the envelope. So, I did, it was a vile of drugs in the envelope. I was pissed because I'm a fast driver, the cops already know my car so if I had gotten pulled over, I would have been locked up for life.

I got back home walked in the house, didn't say a word to her, nor did I hand her anything. I was waiting for her to ask.

She must have known I knew and did not say a word. Time went by she was kind of looking at me trying to feel me out. Eventually, I threw the drugs at her while yelling at her about her addiction, and putting me in harm's way, stealing my money, not to mention letting the dealers use my car. She tried to explain, but she couldn't lie out of this one. Needless, to say we broke up, but we needed each other to pay the rent.

I'm not sure if Dinna couldn't accept, we were no longer a couple or if she couldn't accept the fact, she could no longer use my car. Either way I learned she was keeping tabs on me. I was unaware she borrowed our neighbor's phone whom I went to college with and was eavesdropping on my phone conversations. I could never figure out how she knew my whereabouts, and that I was talking to a young lady who also attended Stockton.

Dinna would say to me you know Trinity is in a relationship. My facial expressions would be like what are you talking about. She would say this constantly but would never elaborate. Finally, I ran into the neighbor who asked me how much longer we intended to keep her phone. I looked at her puzzled, she said your roommate borrowed my phone and never returned it. I apologized and told her the phone would be returned soon. I hurried in the house because I knew Dinna was not home yet. I ransacked her room and found the phone. This explained how she knew my business. Now I don't know how she knew Trinity was in a whole other relationship which I found out to be true after six years of being in this one-sided relationship.

Dinna and I had many arguments about me not letting her use my car. I would watch her personality change from being calm to her face turning red with anger. My car keys were always with me, being I knew her capabilities.
One day we got into a heated argument, and I put my hands on her. This was the first time I ever laid my hands on a female. What I failed to mention in the earlier chapters is that I had anger issues, that I didn't know how to address, not to mention I denied them.

Most people don't know I have an excellent aim. My friends and I were cutting one day at Tyrone's house, one of my friends jokingly got smart with me and I threw a knife at her. On another occasion, I drove Tyrone home one Sunday evening, we had a heated argument in the car. He got out the car walked in front of the car, I took my foot off the brakes, and the car hit his knee. He looked at me, and if looks could kill, I'd be dead.

In this instance with Dinna, I regret that moment in time, and because I know I have these issues, I will not play fight with anyone for fear my anger will stir up. I do believe in karma, although I slapped Dinna in this altercation, I really treated her mean and nasty on that day. I believe karma came back on me from Trinity. I ended up having Dinna removed from the apartment. When our lease was up, I re-signed the lease, not her therefore making me responsible for the apartment. Dinna's drug habit had gotten worse to where she was stealing, lying, and becoming unpredictable with her behavior. I also found out she was using my social security number for employment. As I stated earlier, she was a wanted felon, and I thought she was working under the table until the state sent me a letter, advising me I was still working while receiving unemployment benefits and owed the State of New Jersey $20,000.00. Because of this debt the State put a judgement against my credit report which prevented me from buying a house until it was paid off. I met with the State and attempted to explain although this was my social security number, I didn't work at the places that were listed in the thick file they had on me.

This was the final straw; it was so bad between us she decided to go stay with her sister a couple of days in North Jersey. While she was gone a former student whom I was close with taught me a valuable lesson. She was in the loop of what was going on, and she also had an addict in her family, so she was speaking to me from experience. She asked me a question: what you are going do when you come home one day and find everything in your house gone. This was an eye opener for me, and I knew she was right. The conversation I had with her years ago has taught me never underestimate the wisdom from someone who is younger than you just because of their age.

After this conversation, I called Dinna's sister and informed her of Dinna's identity theft, and the amount I owed the State, that her sister relapsed and is using drugs again and that she can't return to the apartment to live. Her sister understood, but Dinna wasn't trying to hear it. She thought she could sweet talk me into letting her back into the apartment. Dinna returned to South Jersey and stayed at one of her friend's houses. Dinna was escorted by the Police when she came to move her personal items from the apartment. We did not remain friends after this. Years later she messaged me through Facebook with an update of her life and tried to befriend me. I accepted the friend request for 5 minutes, then deleted her.

After Dinna moved out, I couldn't afford the rent. A lady I would babysit for every now and then knew someone who was looking for an apartment. Tammy came to see the apartment, we hit it off perfectly. Tammy was straight, and it took me a while to tell her I was gay. It took a few months before I was honest with her about my sexuality. She was heated with me for not telling her the truth from the door. She stopped speaking to me for a couple of weeks, not because of me being gay, but for the deceitfulness. Once she got pass it, we were inseparable, her boyfriend moved in with us which made the rent cheaper until we had to start chasing him for the rent. Tammy was the best roommate with a heart of gold and could just warm your day with her crazy jokes. She was honest and held nothing back with her thoughts and opinions of something or someone. She accepted me for who I was, spoiled me with cooking every day or ordering out. She also put me in my place when needed it and gave me the best relationship advice. She told me I was clingy and didn't give Trinity room to breathe. She was correct, and I knew I this, but didn't know how not to be clingy. I was seeking attention, and love that Trinity was not giving. Trinity was more than capable of giving me her attention and blowing up my phone. She showed it whenever I would threaten to leave, or she knew someone else was scoping me and getting my time and attention. But as soon, as I dismissed the other person thinking she would continue investing the energy in our relationship she switched back to her old self. I still played the fool bucking to her schedule. Trinity had a good heart I just wanted a place in it.

Tammy and I eventually went our separate ways. She got sick and had to move where she could be cared after around the clock. I finally got a job in my degree working at a youth shelter on the grave shift, when I got off work I would substitute teach, in addition too, I worked as a mentor a couple days of week in the evening. I was maintaining and decided I was ready to live on my own and moved to Mays Landing NJ.
Tammy got better and was able to get her own apartment in Atlantic City, where I spent most of my time because she always fed me when I came over and would make me take food home from out her freezer. Don't know why because I would bring it back to her for her to cook it for me.

As stated, earlier Trinity and I were in a one-sided relationship for about six years. Trinity was available to our relationship when her girlfriend was out of town. None of my friends ever met her except for Elisha who knew her from Stockton. Elisha never thought Trinity was good for me. We never went on dates or seen in public in my area of town. Looking back, we were on the low. Whenever my friends were having a couple's event, I would show up solo. I started to think people thought I was lying about having a girlfriend for she was NEVER around.

She did teach me however, to admit to myself I didn't like being lonely, needed to be in a relationship and forced me to acknowledge I was seeking love and acceptance in all the wrong people. For whatever the reason, I needed to feel needed and wanted, and know that I could depend on my partner when I was feeling low or needed help with a bill or two. Trinity would offer to help me but never did because her girlfriend at the time controlled her finances, and then the truth would come out about who I was or supposed to be.

God did bless me with a good friend as well as my soror who always came through when I was in need. I met Nona while I was a security guard in the Atlantic City School District. I didn't like her at first, but we grew to be close friends, and we've always had each other's back. When my family treated me shady because of my sexuality her family welcomed me. Whenever I needed a loan all she would ask is when am I getting it back. I kept my word on repaying her on the date I said because I knew I would need again. Now Nona had to adjust to the gay lifestyle, she really didn't like Dinna, and couldn't stand Trinity. She saw something I didn't not to mention Nona was in denial for years I was gay. She was, and still is comical when it comes to my sexuality.

I didn't find security with Trinity and found myself grieving the relationship having to admit we were never going to get married, I needed to move on, and finally get a backbone and put my feelings above hers. I knew she loved me, but not the way I needed to be loved. I no longer could stay the side chic. I eventually caught a clue and ended the relationship. We remained friends and touch base from time to time. After my relationship ended with Trinity. I remained single for a while. I was attending a Women's group in Philadelphia on Friday's that met once a month. I met a lot of friends in this group, and we became good friends and hung out outside of the Friday groups. It was in this group I met my bff, and lifelong friend Boo#123456. It was also in this group that I met Elaine, a woman who loved me dearly. So dearly she and I became domestic partners who was best friends with Boo#123456.

Whenever there was an event Elaine was always my date. She was single, and as I stated earlier Trinity was ghost and was never available, so it was a perfect fit for Elaine and me to accompany each other. I remember a group of us were walking down 13th Street in Philly and she shows me her blue bra, she stated it was her lucky bra. Everyone started laughing. If you knew Elaine, she had a great since of humor. She and Tammy shared this trait of bringing joy in people's lives. Tammy and Elaine got along very well. Tammy would call Elaine my old head because Elaine was 10 years older than me.

I remember my first date with Elaine. She got lost looking for my apartment because she was really looking for a farm instead of the store which was called Country Farms. She talked about my directions the entire date, we always looked back and laughed at that memory. We went to New York to have dinner and walk around. I remember Boo#123456 calling to check on Elaine and learned we were on a date in New York, boy was she surprised. She told Elaine she moved fast, we all laughed. After this date Elaine and I spent a lot of time together. Elaine was madly in love with me. I wanted to take it slow because I had to breathe from just coming out of the one-sided relationship I was in with Trinity. Elaine respected my wishes, but that didn't stop her from showering me with her love. I wasn't used to this feeling. When it came to women, I was always doing the chasing. It felt strange for someone to really want and love me outside of the chick I was messing with in college who made Trinity jealous and straighten up and fly right for only a minute. See, I always knew how to give love but never knew how to accept love in my relationships.

Eventually, I became more comfortable with Elaine and she and I, lived together in NJ the year of 911 took place. Our relationship was good. Elaine was quiet and didn't get upset much, but when she did, I knew to shut up and back off. She had this stern look, and I knew to shut up, and leave whatever we were discussing alone. Elaine was a faithful believer in God. She told me from the door she attends church, and no one would come between that. I respected that and attended church with her. We would be in church all day on most Sundays for two services. I'm not going to lie it could be tiresome at times, but it came with the relationship. Eventually we changed churches, but the church rules did not change.

Elaine and I didn't celebrate the holidays together. My family still wasn't accepting of me being gay, and she was not welcomed to my family's house. Each holiday dinner would be at a different family members home.

Elaine would celebrate the holidays with her daughter, and Boo#123456 family who loved her no matter who Boo#123456 were dating. I didn't have the courage to stand up for Elaine or any of my partners. After all it was my family's house, and I had to respect their wishes. On the other hand, I was a punk, and feared my family, and didn't stand up for myself or my partner. Noticeably, I understood it was my family's home, but I could have made a conscious decision to spend at least one holiday with my partner and her family. Looking back, I recognize how she must have felt.

My mom couldn't stand Elaine, to the point she would call me at work and somehow, she would bring up Elaine and call her all types of bitches. I let my mother speak her piece but her hatred for Elaine bothered me deeply, and more importantly, I was either too scared to stand up for myself or was trying to keep the peace; after all I didn't live with her.

My mother expressed her hatred for my friends without getting to know them. She automatically assumed they were gay. One year my cousin had a cookout, and I invited my Soror Nona. My mother and aunt were nasty and rude towards her. Nona never cared for my mother after meeting her. It wasn't until I told my mother Nona was straight that she started being polite to her. The damage had been done, but Nona loved my dad as did everyone. Elaine and I became engaged and were Domestic Partners for about six years. We had a big, beautiful wedding. My family was invited but none showed. Didn't bother me because I always felt my friends were my family, and they showed up along with a few of my sands. Nona was my coordinator who did a great job for someone who had never attended a gay wedding. Till this day she says she had the best time ever and enjoyed meeting the guests.
Not to long after I was hired for the Camden Board of Education SBYS. My coworkers adored Elaine and always came to her defense no matter what I said.

As years went by Elaine became extremely ill. So ill she was unable to work any longer. Things became overwhelming with going to work, calling to make sure she was taking her meds as well, as hoping her sugar wouldn't drop while I was at work. One afternoon I was calling and couldn't get an answer. I called our apartment complex, and they went to check on her.

She had misplaced the phone and they helped her to find it. I so loved that apartment, and the people who worked in the office. Another time my fear came true. I came home from work to find Elaine laying on the floor in the bedroom on the side of the bed passed out. Her sugar had dropped, and I gave her an injection with the EpiPen.

She was rushed to the hospital, and it was then I decided this was too much for me and wanted out of the marriage.

She agreed, and she moved into our second bedroom. The breakup was before the above incident. Elaine assumed I was seeing someone else from a phone conversation I was having one day in the living room. She became so jealous and was chasing me around the living room table calling me disrespectful and yelling hussy to the person on the phone. The funny thing is I was talking to my brother Richie. He was cracking up saying just tell her who you're talking too. I was like no because she will take this position know matter who I'm talking too. Until this day he always brings this memory up, and we crack up laughing.

For the record I didn't just leave my helpless wife. Her health was always my priority, even after her family moved her out of the apartment. I still made sure she had her meds, checked on her during the night, accompanied her to all her scheduled medical appointments, that I scheduled. I would never leave her to take care of herself because she couldn't. It was then her family started coming around and picking her up on the weekends, and soon after moved her into her sister's house in Philadelphia.

While still living with Elaine, my bff's invited me over to her house one Sunday. When I arrived, there was a young lady there with brown eyes, and a nice smile. She was my bff's girlfriend's best friend. The invite was for me to be introduced to Nu-Nu. Nu-Nu is 16 years older than and I. Nu-Nu had beautiful eyes and appeared to be nice. She was also curious about the gay lifestyle. We hit it off and started dating. She also had a daughter who just turned two a couple of weeks before we met. Munchkin loved me at first sight, I remember she couldn't stop playing with my watch, and she stayed up under me. I never dated anyone with a child that young. I became attached to the Munchkin and treated her as if she were my own.

Not that many months passed before Elaine died. Prior to her death, her family would not allow me to see or speak with her. Boo#123456 kept me up to date with Elaine's health, and she would inquire information from me if the family didn't know something about her health because the family refused to ask me anything that would help with Elaine's health and medical history. I have some resentment for her family. Although she and I weren't together, I never stopped caring about her health and spent a lot of time setting her up with the best of services in New Jersey. I had to come to the realization God knew best.

I remember like it was yesterday on a Friday around 2pm. Boo#123456 called me and stated it didn't look good for Elaine, and that the family agreed I could come say goodbye. I was really saddened by this news and my coworker Nei and her friend came with me to say my goodbyes. I knew how to get to the nursing home like the back of my hand, until this day I wonder how I missed that turn. While making a U turn, Boo#123456 called me at 6:06 and said she passed. I was literally around the corner. When I arrived the family really didn't have too much to say to me except for her dad, but they did give me a private moment with her to say my goodbyes. My entire work family who loved her dearly attended her services.

After asking Nu-Nu three times to marry me she finally said yes. Now I really wasn't expecting her to agree on the third time, but for whatever the reason she did. Truthfully, I was just playing, went along with it since I asked several times. My work family had a long intervention with me trying to talk me out of it. I was so mad with them that day. My bff said she didn't introduce us for me to marry her.

In 2008 we had a Civil Union it was a small hot August wedding. My mom attended this wedding along with my family from SBYS who participated in in our wedding. My brother Richie, who I can always count on, was one of my groom's men.

Our wedding started two hours late waiting for her brother to arrive to walk her down the aisle and ended three months later while on our family getaway in Orlando Florida, she announced she wanted out of the marriage, that it was a mistake, and she didn't believe she is gay. I clearly remember Nu-Nu sitting in the bathroom of our beautiful time share she made me purchase saying to me this might be my karma for me leaving Elaine. I thought about it and had to agree.

I was so hurt and embarrassed, I didn't want to hear I told you so after my coworkers had given me that long intervention, my bff had her opinion of course about the marriage. I had no one else to blame but me, along with I charged the wedding, we were supposed split. This truly was a lesson learned. I remained in Munchkin's life after the breakup, while Nu-NU attended college until she returned to live in Trenton. The best thing that came from our marriage was Munchkin, and our dog Socks. Yes, Socks became the family addition, I never wanted. Nu-Nu just had to have a dog. I was opposed to the dog, but Nu-Nu paid me know mind. Nu-Nu's mom knew a lady who wanted to get rid of the dog she got for her son, the son couldn't take the dog because he had a pitbull. We were only supposed to go look at the dog. We looked alright, right into Blackwood NJ. Socks didn't take to Munchkin, he bit her in the face twice. Nu-Nu was ready to get rid of him, Munchkin and I begged her not to, and she agreed. When we separated, she left Socks with me. To this day she says Socks is the best gift she ever gave me, and I concur.

Although separated we remained married for six years because I felt as though she ended the marriage, she should pay for it. We both started seeing other people. I didn't have a problem with the dude she was seeing, but Nu-Nu had a problem with who I was seeing.
Which caused a problem with me getting Munchkin on the weekends. I had Munchkin one weekend and took her with me to see someone I was dating. Munchkin had a ball at the chick's house and was in a safe environment. Hell, I was dating a cop, Munchkin was really safe.
Well, when I told Nu-Nu where we were, she hit the roof, cussed me out, and wanted me to bring Munchkin home NOW!!!!!
Nu-Nu felt as though I should have told her where we were going. I disagreed because I had raised Munchkin, and she knew I would never put Munchkin in harm's way. Munchkin

went on several trips with me and my family, I thought Nu-Nu trusted me to know I would never put Munchkin or any child in harm's way.

Nu-Nu stopped me from getting Munchkin on the weekends. Whenever I would call to get her, her response would be she would have to think about it and get back to me. I would call her back to ask her decision, she would always say something came up, or she's going with her dad.

After several months of these responses, I stopped asking, and stopped calling unless it was her birthday.

Chapter 5
On the Prowl

The cop and I lasted for about a year. She broke up with me just before Thanksgiving. You would think I hated Thanksgiving, after being dumped twice close to Thanksgiving.

It was then my bff talked to me about how I need to stop running from one relationship to the next and learn how to spend time with myself, date myself, and heal. I will admit at the time of this conversation I didn't want to hear what she was saying. But it was the best advice she could have ever given me. I didn't take her advice right off the back, but I did take heed a month or two later.

I never liked being alone, and still don't. I started going out with myself to movies, and dinner, and I learned how to go on getaways with myself. I was enjoying life. It was on a Sunday afternoon after church I went to Hooters for lunch. While waiting for the waitress I was on Facebook and decided to look on one of my friend's pages who had been sick and messenger her. I noticed she was having a conversation with a young lady who apparently was coming out of a relationship and was hurt because she was saying she would never get into a relationship again. Ya'll already know I gave my input into the conversation, and I noticed the conversation went ghost. So, I went on the chick's page my friend was talking with and requested her as a friend. It was something about her profile picture that intrigued me.

She accepted off the bat. I started following her post, but I never wrote anything on her page. January 1, 2013, she posted she was going off the grid, and if someone wanted to talk, they knew how to hit her up. I immediately inboxed her and said I don't know how to hit you up. She responded back with her phone number. I didn't call her right away. I waited a week or two before hitting her up. She didn't answer when I called and didn't respond to my call for another week. She hit me on a Saturday. We talked and shared information about ourselves. She was getting sleepy and said she would call me back. I waited another two weeks for the return call. I knew she had two boys, so I thought she called me on the weekends they were at their dad's house. That was not the case, I later found out she wanted to make me sweat.

After that we spoke all the time, we still never met in person. Finally, she asked me out on a date. We agreed to meet at the bowling alley in Philly. We met up at the bowling alley, she took the bus because her car was not running. Later, I discovered she lived down the street from the bowling alley. I told her I would have picked her up. She was like no, I don't know you like that. We had a great time that night, after bowling I dropped her off at Sisters a women's club on Philly. She thanked me for the ride and gave me a kiss on the lips. She swears she was trying to kiss my cheek, but I turned my head, lies, lies, lies!!!!!!

Valentine's day was coming up she asked me to be her Valentine. I immediately said yes. I found myself buying a Pandora bracelet for someone who is just supposed to be a booty call. She also got me some nice stuff, as well and made me a basket surrounded by rose pedals. No one had ever done this for me. She put a lot of thought into my gift, I loved it. We had nice dinner, as well as a nice evening into the next morning. That morning we had breakfast at the high price

IHOP. I spent a lot of my spare time with someone who was just supposed a booty call. It was something about her, I didn't know what though.

My birthday was coming up. We were at the mall one day and I showed her what my taste was in Guess watches, trying to give her some ideas of what to buy me for my birthday. We celebrated my birthday with her family. Her sister and mom cooked dinner for me at her sister's house. She gave me my gift before dinner. Tanisha is one to never wait to give you your gift she must do it right after she has purchased it. I opened my gift, and it was a Guess watch, however, it was not the watch I picked while we were out shopping, and my face showed it. I told her I liked it, but I needed a link removed from it. She knew I didn't care for the watch and was very hurt by my ungratefulness. I remember she laid on her sister's floor hurt, as well as what she was wearing a multicolored pink and black shirt with black pants. I will never forget how my arrogance that I didn't recognize at the time, could scar someone who was just trying to make my birthday special. She agreed to take it back and give me the money to purchase the watch I wanted. I like a fool was looking on the Guess website looking for another watch for her to order online. That night I never thought to take her feelings into consideration, her time for going to pick out a watch, or the joy I took from her to make my birthday special. Her family wasn't so happy with me either. My arrogance never took into consideration how much I hurt her, and she has never gotten over it and has never purchased me a gift out right again. She gave me a gift card to buy my watch and has continued to give me a gift card when giving me a gift to guard her heart.

I apologized to her back then for being an ass and have continued to apologize to her all these years later, but she has not let it go. This was the start and has continued to be trouble in our relationship. It has taken me some years, but I've learned you can really damage a relationship when not taking someone's thoughtfulness, and sensitivity into consideration due to your own arrogance. Our relationship had many complications. If I had to describe Tanisha's personality, she is someone who needs to feel needed, and must help others. I believe I was different than the other females she was used to being with, my strength, or arrogance, had me thinking I didn't need anything from people not to mention this was how I was raised.

Although we were each other's booty call there was something there. Tanisha made our relationship complicated because she would ignore me, stop taking my calls. It was on a Sunday that she finally answered the phone and explained the situation, she stated her friend who was an ex had cancer she needed to help her. I understood her taking the friend to appointments, and helping her, but what did this have to with us. She further stated she has a calling from God that she needs to answer. I responded I don't have a problem with that either. I had to convince her we didn't need to stop seeing each other for all these things to transpire. She agreed we started spending more time together on the weekends, but I still didn't meet the kids.

A little time passed before her aunt passed on her dad's side. I attended the funeral. Upon walking in the church, Will our oldest son was coming from the bathroom looked at me and knew who I was. We introduced ourselves to each other and proceeded upstairs to the service. I stayed for the repast and mingled with her family. The one thing I will never forget about the repast was Will's plate. That boy's plate was piled sky high, and he ate it all. I was wondering did she feed the boy.

After meeting the boys at the funeral, I started going to Tanisha's house on regular. I stopped pass every Sunday after church and she had my plate either waiting or she was finishing up cooking dinner. I failed to mention this chick can cook her ass off.

I remember always looking in her refrigerator, and freezer it was just about empty. I asked her what the boys were going to eat during the week. She replied she goes to the store each day to get something or else they will eat the food up. In my head that didn't make sense, but I went along with her story. Time is going by. It seems were doing good, and out of nowhere she stops talking to me again. She's not taking my calls, ignoring my text nor is she calling me. So, I started calling her job, she would come to the phone sometimes and say she is busy and hang up, other times she would have her friend who was the manager tell me she can't talk right now. I would call her sister to try and make sense of Tanisha. She would say that's how she is and let her be.

My next attempt was I went to visit her at work. She was shocked to see me, I saw a smirk on her face, and she dismissed me. I spent my time speaking with her friend the store manager. I called her one last time, she answered. I told her I was going to leave her alone and that she needed help, and when she gets herself together to call me. I think this was when I noticed she cared; she was like you going to leave just like that. I explained I have no choice, your personality switches, one minute you want to be bothered, the next minute you're treating me like I don't exist. This situation was messing with my sanity. She didn't want to agree, but she did. Thinking back on the phone conversation, I think she felt as though I was abandoning her.

Well, it didn't take long for little Miss Missy to forget about me, I would call her to keep in contact. She was short with our conversations. If someone was calling her, she hung up with me. I would see her on Facebook flirting with other people. It appeared as though she moved on with her life. Now I'm mad because I stopped seeing her for to get herself together, not see other people. Once I saw she was not working on herself and making it plain on Facebook for me to see she was flirting and moving on to the next, I tried to come back in her life. She wasn't trying to give me the time of day. Her response was I left the relationship and she moved on. I could never get her to understand my reasoning.

One night I was in Philly, it was late I called and told her I was stopping by before I head back to NJ. She was nice, she had a plate waiting for me to take home, all the while she was on the phone talking to someone not giving me the time of day. I had to keep interrupting her phone conversation for her to acknowledge I was there in the house right in front of her. She told whomever to hold on and said, "you ended the relationship so what do you want from me?" I didn't respond, I just left. I called her again a couple of days later to find out if she wanted to attend the poetry slam with me for pride. She replied she would think about it. I started calling her again, and she started ignoring me again. She wouldn't answer my text or speak to me. I called her job on the day of the event, she did speak with me to tell me she wasn't going and hung up. This is when I knew I felt something for this chick, I was hurt.

I was telling my coworkers what she was doing. Now they all agreed she liked me, and interesting enough they liked her. My SBYS family were usually on point. I still wanted to attend the event but was hurt that I would be attending the poetry slam without her. Well, since she didn't want to go, I called my ex, the cop. She accompanied me to the show we took a few pictures before entering the jam, and while in attendance. I enjoyed the poetry, but wasn't into my date, and she wasn't into me. She was on her phone texting her girl which I found out later was a member of my church who seems to want everyone I was with. But that's another story within itself. I kept looking at my phone like someone was going to call me. There were a few acquaintances at the Poetry Jam for me to intermingle with to get my mind off Tanisha.
I went into to work the next day I was showing Nei, and Richie the pictures from the show, and updating them on who I took with me in place of Tanisha. I further stated to them Tanisha was not taking my calls or text. Nei suggested I post a few of the pictures of me and the cop on Facebook, and she stated let's see how fast she contacts you. Ten minutes hadn't passed before my phone rang. You guessed it, it was Tanisha going off on me about if I'm trying to get with her why I would go out with my ex, and she saw the pictures on Facebook. I had her on speaker, Richie, Nei, and I are cracking up because Nei's plan worked.

After that day she no longer ignored my calls, we were going out on dates. Then I received a call from her one day asking what day our anniversary date is. I'm like huh, she repeated herself. I caught the clue she wanted a to make our relationship official. My response was what's today's date. I looked at the calendar it was May 3, 2013, our anniversary date. We were together a little over a year in February before Tanisha and Reese moved to NJ with me. It was an adjustment for everyone. Will didn't move in with us. He stayed with associates and would come visit and stay a while from time to time. Reese hated NJ; all he would say is he didn't ask to come to NJ. He didn't like it. The schools were different in NJ verses for Philly. Ya'll don't know how tired I was of him saying that to us. It wasn't until he met two boys in his eighth-grade class that also lived in the complex before he stopped saying he didn't ask to come to NJ. Too this day they are best friends.

One day Tanisha and I were chilling in the living room. I received a phone call, I didn't recognize the number, so I was hesitant to answer the phone, but something said answer. I picked up and the person on the other end introduced herself as Pamela. She stated where she was from and she was calling from California, I put her on speaker phone. She stated there was someone looking for me and she wanted to know would I be willing to meet them. I immediately replied no, and further stated my life was good, all my exes knew how to contact me, and I'm findable; I can be found on Facebook. She explained this person is not trying to come in between my wife and family. She ended the conversation by asking me to think about it, and she would call me back in a couple of days.

After hanging up the phone Tanisha and I discussed it. I was still saying no because I felt as though my life was full enough with the people that were involved in it. Tanisha felt differently, and wanted me to agree, just to be nosey.

A few days passed and Pamela called back. I told her I would agree to meet this person. She told me the person I was meeting had a busy schedule, and we would have to work around their schedule. I asked where the meeting would take place. She responded it could be in my home, a restaurant, I replied a restaurant would be nice, after all I don't know these people. She informed me there was some paperwork that I needed to sign, and she would fax them to me. Upon going to work I received the paperwork and was reading over it while telling the story to my coworker. While filling out the paperwork I came across a section where I thought it said I had to pay. I immediately stopped doing the paperwork, and laid it on my desk, and I never heard from Pamela after that.

Tanisha and I became engaged on May 7th, 2015, at the bowling alley in Philly where we had our first date. I was hiding her engagement ring which sat in this huge, beautiful box for a month before I could come up with a plan to ask her to marry me. It wasn't until she called me one day at work and said her two best friends were in town and they wanted to meet up. My response without any hesitation was no, only because I knew I didn't have any money I had just bought her ring, and we were leaving for Vegas in two weeks. I could tell she was a little upset with my response.

JUST BEYOND THE BRIDGE

Now my SBYS family knew my plans to ask her to marry me and tried to assist with a romantic way to propose to her. I went into Richie's office and told him what was going on. He said suggested to propose to her while her friends were visiting. I started thinking, and in went on Facebook to inbox Birdie, Tanisha's best friend and told her my plans and explained my reasoning for saying no. She asked me where our first date was, I responded we went bowling in Philly. She replied that's where we would meet up. I so loved this plan. I told Richie the plan he didn't know if he could attend on short notice but helped me put a playlist together of our favorite songs to put on the screen at the bowling alley. I blew up my bff's phone until she answered explaining the plan. She stated she would be a little late but would be there. The plan was coming together. On our way the bowling alley, I told Tanisha my bff and her friend were coming. After all, my bff loves to bowl. Tanisha responded you know she ain't coming because she always makes plans with you, and cancels. In my head I didn't argue with her because of what was taken place. My bff would not disappoint. We arrived at the bowling alley, I passed off the ring to Birdie, one of her besties, and we went inside and got a spot. Tanisha was caught up in catching up with both her besties, she had no clue of what was going on. When my bestie arrived, I met her at the counter which gave me the opportunity to give the play list to bowling manager for when the time came for the special moment.

My bff and her friend met Tanisha's besties, and everyone hit it off well. We started bowling everybody was mingling, I cued for the playlist to start playing. Now Tanisha was so busy talking to her bestie long nails she wasn't paying attention. I had to tell long nails to follow the script. I went over to Tanisha and told her to look up at the screen. While she was reading the screen, which asked the question" Tanisha Laquell Williams Will You Marry Me, I was on one knee with the ring box opened, when she turned to look at me, she looked down and saw the ring, and said Yes!!!!!! After that no one was really into bowling except my bff.

On the ride home Tanisha was excited and immediately set our wedding date for May 6, 2017, a destination wedding, the boys were excited as well. We started searching for different destinations and were scheduled to go to Punta Cana in a couple of months, and we discussed gathering more information on destination weddings while we were there to get a better understanding.

August came and we arrived at Breathless in Punta Cana. We were feeling this spot. While visiting I inquired about a destination wedding. We were given a tour of the different areas we could get married. We selected a beautiful spot overlooking the beach. It was so gorgeous, Tanisha and I started thinking this was the spot for us. After discussing it we decided to make Breathless Resorts our destination for our wedding.

We returned home from our beautiful vacation. A few weeks later we started mailing out "Save the Date" cards, along with contact information for the travel coordinator who was assigned to assist with booking travel for the intended guest. While this process was in development, I got to thinking to myself, we should get married next year, and the following year would be our big wedding at Breathless. Most destinations prefer you be married in the United States, then have the ceremony in the country of your choice. My thought process wasn't farfetched, and I eventually discussed my idea with Tanisha who stated she was thinking the same thing. Since we both agreed to move up our wedding, the date has now changed to May 3, 2016, which fell on a Tuesday. Now, I felt this wedding only needed three additional people in attendance: the boys Tanisha's mom, and Richie. We needed a person to stand up for each of us as our witnesses. Well, this was not the case, Tanisha started a wedding list, I kept saying no to everyone that was on the list and reminding her we have a huge wedding to pay for as it is. As usual she was not listening. We ended up canceling the destination wedding and decided to travel to Breathless the following year for our honeymoon. We made sure the few guests who started paying on the wedding received a refund. A few guests were upset, but wounds were mended before the wedding. From there I started planning our wedding.

Our wedding fell on a Tuesday, I must admit I didn't think then so many would be in attendance on a workday. What I realized after our wedding outside of those who were close to me such as my sorors, and a few personal friends. Most of the guest weren't happy for Tanisha and I and were secretly hoping our marriage did not last. Not to mention a few were jealous and wanted my wife. A few guests came so they could have something to talk about, and not for well wishes. Both my sons walked their mother down the aisle. My brother Richie, and my bff stood alongside me, and long nails, and glamour girl stood alongside Tanisha, and my Momma from church was my Mom for the day, and still is. If have to say so myself, we had a beautiful wedding.

Six months into our marriage, October to be exact, I had to have surgery. My wife was supportive coming up to the surgery, and during the surgery. After my surgery I couldn't return to work until January and had a lot of time at home. I figured with all this time off, my wife and I would do a few getaways on her days off, I thought wrong. After I returned home from the hospital, I spent most of my days on the couch in the living room. Now on this couch is where I observed my wife was changing. Instead of her catering to my needs like I thought she would, she did the opposite.

Let me paint the picture for you. We lived in an apartment on the second floor. Our sofa sat against the back wall, if I look to the left, I could see who's coming in the house, if I looked to the right, I could see down the hall to our bedroom. Tanisha would come in the house, walk to our bedroom change her clothes, and then leave out. To be fair some days she was going to work, and some days she would not come home after work. What I found myself doing is sitting on the sofa for a few weeks turning my head left to see her come in the house, then turning my head right watching her go into the bedroom. This became a pattern, I eventually asked her what was going on.

At first her response was I need time for myself and need to be alone, and she would not look at me. I talked to her best friend about it, and mine. Both were like give her the time and space. I will be honest; I did try, but that was not working for me. We are married, how much time and space did I need to give? Tanisha started attending and joined her besties church, so ya'll already know I started going too. It seemed like this was the only way to get quality time in with my wife until we started taking separate cars.

Well, I decided to plan a getaway and thought this might help our relationship. My wife loves getaways, and I knew this might help the situation and get us to talking again. I even invited her best friend long nails and her partner Boo#123456. I booked a room for us in Cape May at a bed &breakfast that way she would be able to spend time with her bestie, if she got tired of me, not to mention my Boo#123456 would be with me. Everyone was on board except Tanisha. She first stated she wouldn't be able to get off from work which was a little suspicious because every vacation we have had ever taken she took without pay. I suggested she ask for the time off anyway. About a week later she was finally home, and I went into the living room to discuss with her the getaway plans. She stated she was not going, and that she had plans that weekend. I asked her how you have plans knowing what I'm planning with our friends. She looked at me while I was sitting on the arm of the sofa and responded go without me. I was taken aback when she stated this, I knew there was something wrong with my wife.

I immediately went into our bedroom, closed the door got on my knees and prayed for God to fix my wife. As I was coming up off my knees God responded join the church. I responded to God I can join the church later; I just need you to fix my wife. About three days later I was in the bathroom sitting on the toilet I heard God say again join the church. I always heard the old folks God ain't gonna ask you to do something, but so many times. I called Boo#123456 and told her on Sunday I will be joining the church. We both agreed to inform each other when we made our decision to join. She responded she was thinking the same thing and was going to tell me. Sunday came, and I was obedient to God and joined the church.

Now she and I are members of the same church, she sat on one side of the church, and I sat on the other. She was so hostile towards me. I didn't know why. When trying to talk with her, she would reply she was done talking, and that she has been telling me how she felt for a long time, and that's there's nothing to discuss. She also stated that I belittled her, I didn't treat Will right, I didn't satisfy her in bed, and she needed to be free. Know I was shocked about not satisfying her in bed. When we first met, she wasn't complaining, I couldn't get in the front door good, and we were at it, and we weren't serious with each other.

I'm looking at her so hurt and trying to figure out where all this was coming from. All I knew I wasn't trying to lose my wife. She advised me to move on with my life, I replied no, I asked what if we get back together. She replied we are not getting back together, and that she will be moving out at the end of the month. My neck still turning right and left waiting for her to come home and leave back out.

The house was becoming depressing, I decided to go visit Lady my work wife. I could always be honest with her about everything that goes on in my life. She always stayed at work late, so I didn't have to rush the details to what was going on at home. While sitting there I got an alert from the bank. I received an alert money had been paid out our joint account.

JUST BEYOND THE BRIDGE

I checked to see what was paid out, come to find out Tanisha was trying to get an online Attorney to assist with filing for a divorce. I was devastated, and thankful at the same time I was not home by myself reading this information. Lady consoled me all she could, but that tight pain that was in my chest, and the instant headache I got was overwhelming. I drove home in a daze hoping Tanisha would be home so we can talk about her trying to get a divorce, but she was not home when I arrived. I called her about the divorce papers, she replied I told you I wanted out, and she further stated she is moving out on December 30, 2016th.

Well, it was time for our getaway. As promised Tanisha did not come, but the three of us went. We had a great time outside of me being in beautiful huge room by myself. I did, however, acknowledge Tanisha wherever we went. For example, we were always seated at a table set for four. It appears I was always sitting next to the empty chair, and I would say Tanisha you know what you want to eat, and I would really wait for a response, and then reply gurl you a cheap date tonight, we all laughed, and I did this all weekend.
Upon completion of our weekend, we left after breakfast for us to be able to get to get to church on time.
Long nails texted me with a song entitled "God Got A Blessing" the song has a positive message that I hold so dear to me even now.

December 29th came, and Tanisha moved out, after she moved out, I spent a lot of time in church, and over Boo#123456, and long nails house. They were a great support system. I will always be grateful to long nails for teaching me how to pray, fast, and trust God.

This was the start to how God changed my life. God used Tanisha to change my self-righteous ways. When Tanisha and I met I was arrogant, prideful, and thought I knew it all. I didn't care how I spoke to her or other people, I had sympathy, but no empathy. These were some of the things she complained about during our marriage, but I could never see it.

I was raised to believe my family was better than other people and that we were a perfect family, I saw myself as a good person, and my family didn't have the issues that other families had. Now that idea is contradictory to what I thought about my family. One of the reasons I became a Social Worker was because I was the only child, I was a people person, had a listening ear, I'm nosey, and wanted to help people their problems, not ever recognizing that with all my self-righteousness I needed help myself, and so did my family from being so judgmental.

I enjoyed being around my friend's families. It appeared their families were fun, non-judgmental, knew how to laugh and have fun. When being around my family I was extremely uncomfortable like I didn't belong. I'm not sure at what age in my adult life that I prayed not to become like my mother. It wasn't until my boss prophesied to me that I had prayed for something, and God is answering your prayer. I was trying to figure out what prayer she was referring to. I had prayed so many prayers waiting for God to answer. A few days later it came to me I asked God not to let me grow old and become like my Mom.

It wasn't until I got up in my forties, and Tanisha left me that God made me release the fear of her. I can't say what made my Mom tick. She liked money, and having nice things, which was cool, it was just something missing. At the time I never knew that was not a good look to have. God opened my eyes about myself and things I needed to change, and he made become humble. I started to lean on God more, I built a relationship with God, I leaned who he was, and that he loved me, and had a plan for my life. My testimony then and now is God used Tanisha to save me from going to hell. God knew who to use for me to change. God's plan worked, like he ever had doubt.

What I remember about the test God gave me, it was hard as hell. I had to stand on the promise and keep the faith that God was going to return my wife back to me.
Tanisha kept her distance from me, while God was working on me. But one thing remained true, when she told me she was not coming back, I told her she was. I kept the faith, perseverance, and being obedient to God.
In the first couple of weeks, God led me to a scripture which stated in my terms when you ask God for something ask without motive. I started crying and told God I was asking without motives and didn't understand why he was not answering me.

Tanisha had moved on with her life and was seeing someone else, and with all this being done in front of my face, I knew God was going to return her to me like he promised. Everyone including Tanisha thought I was crazy, and a fool. Tanisha would tell me to move on with my life, and I would respond your coming back to me. She would give this look like you keep thinking that if you want to.
I must admit it was looking like God was not going to answer my prayer anytime soon.

I saw Tanisha at a mutual friend's baby shower. I wasn't going to the shower, and she called me asking why I wasn't there. I jumped up got ready and went to the Shower. She was leaving as I arrived. I asked her if she was happy with the person she was seeing. The way she responded I knew she wasn't happy. I showed her that I took off my wedding band hoping she would care, her response was like that's good. She pulled off and I went into the shower.

Later that evening God took me to certain scriptures in the Bible. One scripture he took me to he advised me to start tithing. The second scripture God took me to he told me to buy a house. I remember calling long nails, and Boo#123456 that Sunday night and saying, I'm going to let Tanisha be, and I'm going to buy a house.

Later I went into the kitchen, and I asked God when he was going to send me a friend. I said Tanisha is seeing someone, and he responded in two weeks. I started thinking about the holidays in the new house and was also thinking Tanisha and her friend could come over to the house for the holidays with my new friend and we could all celebrate together.

That was the turning point. God revealed he was sending Tanisha back in two weeks. God is not a man that He shall lie nor the son that he shall repent. We were apart seven months before God answered my prayer. I remember while trying to select a home, God told me to keep her in the loop with the home selection. I would have Reese take pictures of the homes and he would send them to my wife. She would reply no. Prior to us getting back together, Tanisha asked me how house shopping was going. I responded not well, but I was still hopeful. She suggested I send her the listings of the houses. As she requested, I sent her all the houses the realtor sent to me. Tanisha picked a couples houses she thought I might be interested in. One of the houses she selected, I wouldn't go look at. The house was in the woods. In my head what black people live in the woods. I scheduled an appointment on June 30, 2017, to see the house. I asked Tanisha would she like to come with me and Reese. She replied yes. On June 30, 2017, we put a bid on the house and closed on our home in August 2017.

Chapter 6
Revelation

We moved into our new home, picking furniture, in addition to shopping for our trip to Punta Cana in a few weeks. Life couldn't be more perfect. We had a blast at the Hard Rock Café in Punta Cana. This was Reese senior year in high school, Will was holding it down with working. All was well in our world, we were happy spending a lot of time together, then boom her aunt passed in October of 2018. Anyone who knows my wife knows she does not handle death well at all. Not to mention her aunt passed a month before the holidays, which Tanisha hates because of the timing of several family members deaths around the holidays.

This is where we started to go downhill again. Tanisha became distant leaving the house again staying at her Mom's house, when she would stay at home, she switched from our bedroom to Reese's bedroom. When he would come home from college on the weekends she would sleep on the sofa. Our communication was almost nonexistent. If I asked a question her response would be short, or a smart answer. I was trying to be understanding knowing she was grieving, along with the following month was her normal time to start grieving the loss of her loved ones. But I also notice something else wasn't right. The way she was treating me brought back memories of first time she left me, but I paid it no mind.

Weeks went by with my wife having the same behavior, and me becoming upset. I went work as usual as if nothing were wrong at home. One day I was walking back to my office I saw one my coworkers about to walk up the steps. Now in my head, I wasn't going to stop and talk with her, I was gonna speak and turn to go to my office. She turned came back down the steps to meet me in the hallway. And what she said was "The same thing that happened to you in a certain situation will happen again. She further stated it's a cycle of three. I immediately knew what she was speaking of. She continued to speak on how I would pass the test each time. I learned on this day if God wants to get a message to you, you will not be able to avoid hearing it no matter who God uses. About two weeks later while at work a student came into our office with a nice white jean jacket. I asked him where he bought it from. He responded the jacket cost $8, and he told me the name of the store at the mall.

Once he told me the price, I told my coworker at lunch I'm going to the mall to get that jacket. Well, upon entering the mall God spoke to me and said "Test". Needless to say, the store did not have my size in the jean jacket. I returned to work telling my coworker I wasted my lunch time. I got on my email and noticed an email from my wife she sent on Monday on my day off. I couldn't understand why I was just seeing this email from yesterday after being on my email all day. Anyway, I read the email which read in brief "Ellen, I love you, but I'm leaving you. I feel the need to go help and live with my Mom." I was calm while reading this letter, and remembered the prophesy, and realized this had been prophesized to me two weeks ago, and two years ago to that date my wife left me the first time. I immediately printed out the email and took it to Lady my work wife's office for her to read.

She read the email she looked at me and said, "the Holy Spirit told me to tell you leave her be, or it will be longer". And when she made the statement, she touched me in the same spot the Lord had been touching me, and I knew the Holy Spirt was talking through her. I listened to the Holy Spirt and Lady, and I didn't bother Tanisha unless she called me for something or came to the house. Tanisha moved out of our home in December. I was devastated again, I called Boo#123456 and told her what was going on we spoke for about two hours, then long nails got on the phone to offer words of encouragement, in addition to telling me this was my Trust God season, and God had someone for me.

In January on a Friday evening, I was in the mall shopping for Valentine's Day for my wife because in my head we were celebrating Valentine's Day that year. God started talking to me in the mall and was revealing things to me about people in my family using witchcraft. I wasn't really understanding what he was trying to say to me. Saturday morning God woke me up early and started showing me all the things in the house that came from the old apartment, my mother's house, things of Tanisha's that she held on to for generations and left behind. This is an experience I will never forget. I felt like I was moving all over again. When I moved to our home, my brother Richie built me a closet. God had me throw out a lot of my clothes. For those that know me, know I had a lot of clothes, shoes, sneakers, and coats. God stripped me of majority of my clothes. I threw out years of Delta paraphernalia, elephants, pictures, things that I held dear to me from being online. Items that were brought for Socks from this person. This was a traumatic experience, and I couldn't share it with too many people because not everyone believes in witchcraft, let alone the person who was behind it. During that period, I was able to mention it to two people

Lady, and my coworker who prophesized to me. I was thankful they believed me and didn't think I was crazy.

It took me until March to remove all the curse items I had been carrying for years from several apartments to our home. Not to mention I was wearing the curse, because the curse came from a close relative that I trusted, and never would have imagined they were into witchcraft let alone would curse me. Upon the start of cleaning out our home, I asked God where I was supposed to dump all this stuff. Gods ' response was return it back to where you moved from, and that's exactly what I did.

During the time of this transition, long nails was not lying about me having to trust God. Not only was I tired from all this cleaning, and removing items from the house, I would come home from work and start up all over again. It seemed like a never-ending story God was always saying you missed something especially all the things I was trying to hold on to. I remember arguing with God about the television in our bedroom. God told me to throw it out. I kept saying no and told him I'll throw it out when Tanisha comes back home and can afford a new one like we planned. Gods 'response to me "is the television worth losing your wife". Ya'll already know who won that argument. I threw the large television out and put the smaller television in our bedroom. Added to my stress of worrying about how I was going to pay the mortgage, the household bills, not to mention my personal bills all by myself.

I ended up telling my brother Richie who has been my brother for over sixteen years whom I met at another job.

Richie is the brother I never had being the only child, and truly does take care of me like were blood siblings.

After I told Richie Tanisha left me again, we discussed how I was going to keep the house. We both thought it best if I sold it, I would come out on top, and buy a cheaper house with cash. Tanisha and I shared a phone line. I noticed she was over on a particular day, and she left her phone on the counter. I'm looking at the phone like it could answer wondering why she did that. Not to mention when she left the phone, she didn't give me her new number. I was pissed off, and inboxed her on Facebook stating all we've been through you have the audacity to treat me like a stranger, and not give me your new number. She didn't respond, and I didn't bother to ask the kids what the new number was.

This was the last straw for me. I told God I was done with this chick always disrespecting me and treating me like I did something to her. Not to mention looking like a fool waiting for her to return, while she was publicly seeing someone else. Around about January I called a realtor to discuss selling the house. Tanisha was looking in the security camera and saw there was a man in the house. She called me I didn't recognize the number, so I didn't answer.

She texted me that she was calling me, this is how I got her new number. She wanted to know who that man was that was at the house, and why was he there. I responded what man !!!! she said the white man in the house. I forgot she had access to the camera in the house. I never responded. Several people came to look at the house, but no offers.

JUST BEYOND THE BRIDGE

I was talking to a student in the hall one day and he informed me his parents 'house is up for sale, but it seems no one is interested in buying. In my head I was thinking that's a shame because I know my house is going to sell because the Lord told me to put it on the market. Thinking back, I don't know why that boy told me that story. It might have been God telling me in that conversation my house isn't going to sell either.

Later that day I went to out to lunch to the Chinese restaurant located in Camden on Mt. Ephraim Ave. After I ordered my food, I noticed I had a missed call. I listened to the message and there was a woman calling whose message sounded like I was familiar with her. Oddly, I returned the call. I usually don't return calls if I don't know the person, but it was something about her voice, that made me return the call. I called she picked up and said this is Ellen, you just called me. she replied" Hi, this is Pam I spoke with you and your wife three years ago when I told you that you were adopted". I said honey you never told me I was adopted, and you must have the wrong person. Pam replied your name is Ellen Lindsey correct. I replied yes. She stated you were born in Elizabeth NJ at Elizabeth General Hospital. I responded yes. She continued to say then I have the right person. I asked her when my birthday is. She started looking through her papers. She replied let me call you back in ten minutes. As promised, it was ten minutes exactly. She said your birthday is March 13, I said nope, and in my head, I was like I knew you had the wrong person. Then she said no, its March 14, 1969. She continued to say I'm 99% sure you were adopted. I was in disbelief. I have my food now, and I'm driving back to my office.

She further stated your parents never told you that you were adopted. I answered no. She went on to ask were my parents older. I responded yes. She continued to say she believes one parent was in there 40's at the time of adoption. She asked me were my parents still alive. I replied my dad passed in 2008, and my mom was still living. We ended the conversation with Pam asking would I like to meet my blood family, and would I trust her. I replied yes to both. She stated I would need to take a DNA test, and she would be in touch.

I returned to my office like what the hell!!!!! I immediately called Tanisha. She wouldn't answer the phone, she texted stating she was at work text her. Now I know she was being an ass because any other time you talk at work. So, I started texting her and sent some of the information, while in the middle of the next text she calls me. She's like what the hell! I repeated everything Pam said to me. Tanisha was concerned about my well-being with finding out news like this. We started guessing was my dad my real dad, and my mom adopted me, and now the family is looking for me. Tanisha suggested I call my sister Fran and see if my dad had told her I was adopted. After all she's my older sister who is deceased were the only sibling's I knew I had. She ended the conversation by telling me to pray on it, and let God lead me.

After work I went home and called my sister and told her what happened. She was like what!!!!!!!!!! Are you sure this woman is on the up and up? She told me to look up Pam's information, in case she is a fraud. She continued to say my Dad never mention me being adopted, and this was news to her ears. Frances suggested and I agreed we would not mention this to my Mom or anyone in the family in case it was not true. Fran told me she and her family did the Ancestry DNA test in December when they were offering a special, I was like now you tell me. She stated she would keep a watch for the next time they were running a special. She schooled me on how the test is set up, and how it listed people in the family that was a match to your bloodline.

Lo and behold, my sister calls me stating Ancestry went on sale, and for me to call my niece so she can order the kit for me. The kit came about a week later, I had to put my saliva in a tube shake it and it turns blue. I was nervous, I followed all the instructions, registered it in their system and sent it back. They email you an approximate date for when the results will return. Every week my sister calls me telling me to check my emails because the results will return early like there's did. I was still looking, still no results.

In the meantime, the relator scheduled an Open House almost every Sunday. Finally, someone appeared to be interested in the house and we might have had a buyer. I'm getting excited and thinking about where in the area I and the pets might want to move to next. I was approved for a mortgage and decided I would keep the same realtor to find my next home. While waiting for the phone call saying there's an offer on the house, I was at work headed to the bathroom in the hallway I might add, my boss blurts out stop letting people in your house. I back tracked to the office forgetting I had to go to the bathroom. She repeated herself. Stop letting people in your house. I replied, I must let people in because the house is up for sale. Again, she repeated herself stop letting people in your house, I found myself wondering am I doing the right

thing. Even though my boss works my nerves God has used her in the past for a few revelations. Now I'm thinking.
I'm still in the process of removing the evil from the house and beginning to trust God more while I'm going through this process, and still believing my wife will be returning home soon. I even booked a trip back to Punta Cana, Hard Rock Hotel where we stayed on our last vacation. I remembered the smile on my wife's face the first time we stayed there and knew this would be the perfect spot again.
I received a call again from Frances telling me our cousin got her results back, and I should receive mine any day now so keep looking.

Two days later I received an email with the results. I didn't know how to read this thing. It looked like a map to me, meaning I can't read or navigate a map. So, I did the next best thing and looked for my sister, my nieces, and nephew's names, family members on my mom's side of the family, someone that I can connect with. WAIT!!!!!!!
I don't know any of these people on this list. Is this real, I connect to none of the people I called family my entire life, but to a list of strangers I don't even know. One of the things I used to say to myself when my family was doing somethings, I found to be crazy is that I'm glad I'm not a Smith. Never knowing I really wasn't.

I started inboxing the relatives that were listed as second, third, fourth cousins. There was a cousin listed as my first cousin. I inboxed her really hoping for a response because we were listed as closer in the bloodline. I explained to all who I was and asked how we were related on the family tree explaining I was adopted and knew nothing. A few responded

but were no help to me, however one cousin did inform me she believes I'm on the Saunders side of the family. They all wished me luck, and we became Facebook friends.
Later, that evening I phoned my sister and told her I received the results, and that we weren't blood related, she was as shocked as I was. Frances stated we will always be sister's blood or not. She asked several questions about the people listed on the information giving to me. I read her a few of the names, and like me no one stood out that she knew.
After receiving my results, I called Pam asking for the kit she was mailing to me. She apologized and stated she is dealing with a family emergency, and to give her a week or two to get back to me. I told her I understood and hoped all worked out.

God was moving in ways I never would imagine with getting the bills paid, not missing a beat with the mortgage. Don't get me wrong I was struggling like hell, but God kept me, and our home. I remember the first sign of things were getting better. I ordered a Rib Entrée from TGIF one Sunday for dinner. Now this might sound stupid for some, but for some months I couldn't afford to eat out, and if I did it was because I skipped eating lunch and ordered my dinner from the corner store in Camden. In the meantime, Pam sent me the kit, it was the same kit from Ancestry that I just did, only this time I returned the kit to her.

A few weeks later she called asking me if I did the Ancestry kit already, because my DNA was in the system. I responded yes and gave her my information needed for her to access the information that was required for her.
Pam got back in touched with me about three weeks later to ask my availability to meet my sibling. Just to hear" meet my

sibling" was exciting and fearful at the same time. I informed Pam of my availability requesting to meet my sibling in November so I wouldn't have to use my vacation days. Pam noted my availability and said she would get back to me after speaking with my sibling.

This was leeway to how God started to turn things around for our marriage. In April Tanisha started coming over more and talking about the vacation I booked, without her knowing I booked the trip to Punta Cana with her in mind and she was included in the trip.

We started going out on dates, and she eventually returned home, and in May we celebrated our third wedding anniversary. In the meantime, Pam contacted me again asking if my wife and I would be willing to fly to California to meet my sibling. Pam was on speaker so Tanisha could hear her. We were like yes!!!!!!!

In July we went to the Poconos to celebrate Tanisha's birthday. While there I received a call from Pam asking were we available to fly out to California in August. I responded if it's in the beginning of August yes, if near the end we must decline because we were going on vacation. Pam stated she was trying to get this done before the production crew goes on vacation. She asked are you willing not to go on your vacation. I replied no. She asked not even to meet your family? I laughed and said nope. She said ok. I will see what I can do. Upon hanging up I told my wife I don't think we're going to California this month. She asked why I say that. I responded I just don't feel that we are.

Pam got back to me later in the month and said it couldn't be scheduled for August. About a week before it's time for us to leave for our vacation my Mom's aid calls me and stated my Mom was rushed to the hospital. I left work and went up to the hospital. Upon arrival she was in the emergency room talking with her aid who is more like family than an aid. I sat down trying to get the 411 of why she's in the hospital when the nurse comes in and interrupts the conversation in a good way. Somehow the subject got on breastfeeding. The nurse was pregnant with her second child and began discussing how hard it was for her to breast feed. Then my Mom joins in on the conversation and says she tried to breastfeed me, but I wouldn't take to it. Now in my head I'm trying to figure out how that happen when you didn't birth me. So now I'm getting anxious to the point I want the truth because something is not adding up.

I texted Pam and told her the conversation that was taking place. She told me to ask my mom about being adopted, and maybe she would tell me the truth. My wife advised me to do the same thing some time ago. But as I told them both I don't think she would tell me the truth. During the conversation via text with Pam I agreed to make myself available the next date that is convenient for my sibling and I will just take off.

About a week after we returned from vacation Pam called and stated my sibling is available in October would I be available. I responded YUP!!! She told me the dates but had to confirm and would get back to me, she ended the conversation stated with we will be airing on the REAL!!!!!!!!

We're in the house screaming, WE GONNA BE ON THE REAL!!!!! We only told selected people we were going on the Real. Pam called us a couple of days later with the exact dates

October 6th-9th 2019. She also gave us the phone number for the producer at the Real because he would assist us from now until the show. I called the producer. We spoke. He asked my wife and I several questions. We also had to send a picture of us, and we had a Face Time conversation where we met the producer and a few of his staff that would be assisting us with our travel arrangements to and from California. They informed us we had to bring several outfits, that were certain colors and dress attire.

We both went to work the next day and requested vacation days for the selected dates. I informed both of my bosses of what was going on and the reason for me taking vacation in October which is unusual for me because I take vacations towards the end of the school year. My boss immediately signed off on it, as well as Tanisha's job.

In mid-September we received our airlines and hotel information, you already know your girl was looking up the hotel amenities for our trip so we would have an idea of what extras to pack.

The day arrived for us to fly out to California were at the airport and so excited. I'm really surprised we didn't go over the fifty pounds. Although Tanisha's suitcase was close to forty-nine pounds, but I'm not gonna lie my shoes were in her suitcase.

OMG the flight to California was long!!!! This was why I hadn't visited there in years. While on the plane Tanisha informed me, she set the DVR to record the REAL while were away, and further stated Tisha Campbell was the guest co-host this week. I was like kool.

JUST BEYOND THE BRIDGE

Our plane landed in California, and we were so excited. We got our luggage and headed out to find our chauffeur who we passed several times. I called him he had me describe to him what we were wearing. He was like look behind you, we felt dumb. He takes our luggage, and we follow him to the car which was a Black Cadillac Escalade courtesy of the Real. We arrived at our hotel. It was small but quaint. Immediately I hung up our clothes for the show we couldn't be wrinkled on television and have people talking about me not mention embarrass my old and new family. At the hotel they had a trolley that took you around the area for free. So, we took a little tour and got off at Disney Land. I never liked Disney Land. It's nothing compared to Disney World. But I wanted to see if it built up much from when I last visited in high school. Which of course it did, but still wasn't better than Disney World. We walked the board walk and discovered they had a Hard Rock Café restaurant which is my favorite, so we grabbed lunch, and watched the sites.

We returned to our hotel on the trolley and noticed there was a supermarket on the same block as our hotel. We got off the trolley walked to the supermarket and picked up some snacks for our room and grabbed dinner from another spot in the same vicinity. After walking to and from the hotel we decided to rest up from our long day not to mention the time change. The next morning arrived and we went to breakfast in the hotel which cost $50.00 for two at the buffet. I booked us an 8-hour tour to see California. It was nice. We toured the many different sections of California. We had lunch at the Cheesecake Factory, to my surprise the price wasn't much different than back home. This was a long fun day, we had a good time, and we were tired.

The day finally arrived that we all have been waiting for. My wife got up early getting herself together, I was still in bed, she's fussing you know the limo is going to be here at 11:00 am and we must be outside when he arrives. I'm like I know and told her I don't want to go anymore. She looked at me with that special look she gives me from time to time and said your just nervous now get up. I looked at her and did as told. We were ready and outside before the limo arrived. We didn't want breakfast that morning, my nerves were already bothering me, and didn't want to be running back and forth to the bathroom.

We arrive at Warner Brother Studios; it looked so much different in person than on television. The chauffer parked the limo and came around to let my wife out first, then came around for me. While he was getting our extra belongings out of the trunk incase, we were asked to change our attire, another limo pulls up, and Pam along with her husband get out of the limo. This was our first time meeting each other, we embraced each other and discussed was I nervous, I said no I'm good. We didn't have much time to chat because we had to go to our separate trailers.

We had a personal attendant who attended to all our needs. Upon entering our trailer, we had all types of snacks, water, soda to make us feel comfortable. They also asked if we wanted a meal and showed us a menu. Neither of us wanted anything nor did we really have time because before we knew it the producer came and introduced himself to us and wanted to know if we had questions for him, in addition to he asked me some refresher questions from him talking to me and my wife on FaceTime. After I answered the questions and reassured him, I was not nervous he told us someone from the set would be coming to drive us to another trailer to get our makeup done. We arrived at makeup; my wife of course didn't need any makeup. She did her own, and it was flawless. I on the other hand they put just a little because outside of our wedding I don't wear makeup.

While we were getting our makeup done, they brought Pam to get her makeup done as well, so we were able to chit chat a little more about our flight and arrival time. My makeup was done, and Tanisha and I returned to our trailer. We're not in the trailer ten minutes before our personal attendant came and said it's showtime. He drove us back to the studio, we got out, and were put in a secluded area. Now my wife was sitting on the sofa, and I was pacing the floor. We were in this spot for a while and could hear the show. Wouldn't you know Tanisha says she has to go to the bathroom, and then going to ask me where the bathroom is. I'm looking at her like I know. We found someone who shows her how to get to the bathroom. Now, I'm more nervous thinking they were going to come get us while she was in the bathroom. She returned before time, and we waited about another ten minutes before they came and got us. She and I were separated, they took her to her seat while I met up with Pam backstage to go on stage. We were told where we each would sit on the sofa next to the stars of the show.

It's a commercial break, they brought us on the stage I sat near Tisha Campbell, Pam is sitting next to me on my left. I was asked how I met Pam, and I explained this was my first time, meeting Pam, and that we always spoke on the phone or via text. I explained that I never knew I was adopted until Pam reached out to me, and the story about how she thought she told me I was adopted during our initial conversation. Pam interjected and explained that initially three years ago when she made the phone call, we were supposed to be on another television show, but the show was cancelled. All these years I thought Pam never contacted me again because I didn't send that paperwork back because I thought I had to pay for something.

Now Tisha starts asking me questions that she barely let me finish the answer to. Tisha asked me how I felt about meeting my family for the first time. "She went on to say she was nervous for me, and continued to say if it was my sister, if it was me, I would be like, I hope she ain't no crackhead. Now while she's saying all this in my head, I'm thinking she need some counseling, and can you just bring my sibling on the stage please. Instead, I said it's strange this is like a dream. All these years I've known who I was raised with, but to find out today I'll meet who's my blood it's kind of like... and Tisha finished the statement by asking would I be happy, I replied yes. That's when she says I'm your sister!!!!!! We hugged each other and broke down in tears. She continued to tell me I have a whole brother who was about to come onto the stage, and she pointed out another brother who was in the audience sitting in the aisle on the other side of my wife. From My understanding my wife met my brother while they were being shown to their seats. In between the commercial break Tisha went and hugged my wife, then returned for the next segment.

They introduce my brother Duan, I met him while he was walking on the stage we hugged for a few minutes, and they made us come sit on the stage. My brother Duan explained he had been looking for me for eighteen years. All three of us were on stage crying happy tears, as well as my wife in the audience. It was a day and a feeling I will never forget.
After the show we went back to my sisters dressing room, where I met her oldest son, my nephew. We're all in the dressing room my wife, and my other brother. My sister Face Times my birth Mom. Tisha and Duan tell her they found me. I saw my birth mom for the first-time boy did she look just like me!!!!!!. We talked a few minutes, and then we hung up, and we called my sister Fran. Everyone welcomed each other to the family.

My sister had to get ready to change and leave her trailer. We agreed to meet up for lunch. The Limo came and took Tanisha and I back to the hotel and we changed our clothes. Tisha sent a Lyft for us to get to the restaurant. Upon our arrival my cousin Arron was there with his two daughters who is my mother's sister's son. I was informed I have six siblings': four brothers, and two sisters. My sister stated I made seven the number of completions.

My brother treated for lunch, and we stayed at the restaurant and talked a while, later my brother drove my wife and I back to the hotel. This was an exciting day, and a day that has changed my entire life. The next day was our departure day, before going to the airport my brother Duan came to our hotel and we went to breakfast, and he answered some of the questions I had like how our parents are, do we have a big family, and more importantly, how did he find out I existed. He told me about a conversation he overheard from one of our aunts stating he would have loved his sister. This is when he started asking questions. He told me my mom has cried for years when my birthday rolls around. I responded she won't have to cry next year. Duan and I exchanged information, he gave me my parents phone number and address.

Upon our returning home, that weekend my wife and I headed to Virginia to meet my birth parents, and another brother Taj. We arrived at Duan's house, and my dad met my wife and I at the door. My dad gave me a big hug, then my wife. Strangely enough, I stood in the kitchen with my dad who I call Pops a good while before I even got to hug my mom. Tanisha, however, was in the living room with my brother and Mom. Eventually, my mom, brother, dad, and Tanisha came into the kitchen and Billy my brother's roommate, and bestie took our pictures. Later that evening my brother Taj arrived, and we also stood in the kitchen talking uninterrupted for about two hours. I believe we stayed two days before heading back home. It was a great welcoming visit from my blood family. We took plenty of pictures but couldn't post until the show aired on October 15, 2019.

Well, after my return from our visit to Virginia I had to visit my Mom who raised me to inform her I know the secret she has carried for 49 years, before the show aired on television. She was not a happy camper. She stated she knew I would find out one day. She further stated when I was younger, we would watch movies when the child would find out there adopted. She stated she asked me would I want to know, and I responded no. I said I don't remember that, but if you say so. She then asked me why I lied and told me that I hurt her by lying to her about the reason my wife and I were going to California. I replied, my sister Frances and I thought it best to make sure this was the truth before hurting her.

She then asked me why didn't the person who found me come to her first. I explained I'm of age they didn't have to come to you and ask you anything. My Mom also asked me why I would want the world to know I was adopted. I was like I didn't mind. She went on to say some hurtful things, she said your mom didn't want you, she just up and left you in the hospital, they couldn't find your father, he didn't want you either. She continued to say my Dad who raised me is probably turning over in his grave. My visit was short, but before leaving I reassured her, she would always be my mother.

The next day my Mom called me demanding the number of Pam, because she had some questions for her. She stated she wants to know how Pam found me because Elizabeth General was close. I told her I was not giving her Pam's number. She wanted to know why. I first said I would ask Pam if she minded me giving my Mom her number. That was fear talking, then I said no. My Mom then asked why. I said there is no reason for you to have her number. The truth is out, and let it be. She then asked me if she asked me some questions would I answer. I replied, you can ask, but that doesn't mean I was going to answer. She gave a sly remark and was like never mind.

Well, It's October 15, 2019. The DVR is set to record the show at home, and I planned to watch it on my phone at work. It about 10:45 I got a phone call to come to the office. I'm like really. I arrived at the office my co-worker said congratulations, the students are trending about you and your sister are about to be on The Real. They were so happy for me. I watched it in my work wife's Lady's office with a few of my co-worker's. Later I found out most of the teachers let the students watch it because they were all watching on their phones. When the broadcast was over, all the love I received from my students, coworkers, and principal was over whelming. The love I received on Facebook from different people who inboxed me telling me they were crying while watching the show, and saying it's hope for them to find their family. I would go to different stores people would stop me, and say you were on the Real, and would congratulate me, and tell me how happy they were for me and my family and how they cried. I was surprised people recognized me because I had changed the color of my hair. This recognition went on for long period of time. I still run into people who find my families story so amazing. My Mom who raised me did watch the show and found fault on my response of how I stated I was raised. She felt as though I should of spoke more about the good life that she and my Dad gave me.

In November, my cousin Gail prepared a Pre-Thanksgiving dinner up in North Jersey for my household family to meet my grandmother Sissy, my great aunts Granny, and Aunt Grace, who are my grandmothers 'sisters, a host of cousins, my aunt Andrea who is my mom's sister.

Gail also prepared a slide show of my family history with pictures of my ancestors. Not to mention she made a beautiful book, with the pictures of the slide show inside. The book sits in our living room on display. My job had a show & tell one day on Zoom, and I showed my book. Everyone loved it. Prior to going to North Jersey to meet my family who are from Rahway, NJ, I met my Great Aunt Doris who was listed on Ancestry as my first cousin. Aunt Doris is my grandfather's sister who was married to my grandmother on my Mom's side. As it turns out my Aunt Doris does not live too far from me. I keep in touch with my family. My wife and I visit Virginia often to see my parents and my brother. In August I went to Virginia to celebrate my Mom's birthday with her and my brother. I speak with Tisha whenever she is not busy, to be honest Tisha, and my brother Duan call my wife more than they call me which is awesome.

I attribute my wife leaving me to the blessings God has bestowed upon me. I told my family, if Tanisha had never left me, they would not have liked me. The year Tanisha left me is the same year Pam contacted me for the first time. My testimony has always been and will always be God used Tanisha's leaving me to change me into who God would have me become. Tanisha was the bait God used to get my attention because I wanted my wife back. God used those years of my transformation taking me to scriptures on how I should be treating my wife, and not letting my mother come between my wife and I. In addition to learning how to listen to her with empathy, the learning how to empathize was hard. You would think me being a social worker I would have already had it. Her leaving me taught me how to be a better Crisis Counselor. I took time to actually listen and hear what my students and families had to say, verses my opinions of the situation. I started attributing what God had done in my life in my counseling sessions and started showing people more grace instead of judgement.

      With cleaning out the house removing the curses that was carried from several destinations to our new home, God was preparing me to meet my loving humble, sincere, God-fearing family. I tell my brother Duan often if my family had met me on the first phone call from Pam, they would have met an arrogant, nasty, never wrong, self-righteous person, and have disassociated themselves from me after our introduction. My brother and I spend several hours on the phone discussing the Bible, and how Good God is. If I don't understand something he explains it to me, we ask each other's thoughts on things of God. Lastly, I can trust him to pray for me, and not on me. God has truly blessed me above measure, and I'm so thankful to God for allowing me to meet and be a part of my blood family's life.

About the Author
Ellen H. Lindsey

Ellen H. Williams-Lindsey is openly gay and a native of Plainfield NJ. She relocated to the South Jersey area in her twenties after her parents bought a home in Manahawkin NJ. Ellen is a member of Delta Sigma Theta Sorority INC. Ellen has worked in the Camden City School District for 16 years. She loves working with young adults, assisting with their development.

Ellen loves basketball, music, and traveling.

ELLEN H. LINDSEY